COOK!

COOK!

MICHAEL LEE-RICHARDS

Foreword by Lyn Hall

photography by
Johannes van Kan

REED

To my mother, Cherry,
for being the very best friend to all her six children,
for her encouragement and quiet faith in us,
and for installing in us all a magical love of life.

First published 1995 by Reed Books, a division of Reed Publishing (NZ) Ltd, 39 Rawene Road, Birkenhead, Auckland 10. Associated companies, branches and representatives throughout the world.

Text copyright © Michael Lee-Richards 1995
Photographs copyright © Reed Publishing 1995

This book is copyright. Except for the purpose of fair reviewing, no part of this publication may be reproduced or transmitted in any form or by any means, electronic or mechanical, including photocopying, recording, or any information storage and retrieval system, without permission in writing from the publisher. Infringers of copyright render themselves liable to prosecution.

ISBN 0 7900 0388 0

Cover and text designed by Clair Stutton
Photographic styling by Gaye Johnson

Printed by Toppan, Singapore

CONTENTS

Acknowledgements	4
Foreword by Lyn Hall	5
Speaking Personally	6
Fabulous Finger Food	20
Astonishing Appetisers & Sensational Soups	42
Extraordinary Entrées	62
Stunning Sorbets & Sumptuous Salads	80
Mighty Mains	102
Disgraceful Desserts	138
Confections with Coffee	162
Back to Basics	178
Glossary	187
Index	189

ACKNOWLEDGEMENTS

If you want to set aside time to write, yet still run a restaurant and catering company, you need an extraordinary staff. I am very lucky to have a great team, and I want to thank them all for making it possible for me to write this book and for keeping the businesses running smoothly while I was slaving away over a hot word processor.

In particular, I wish to thank two very special people. Gaye Johnson did a tremendous job styling the food for the photographs in this book, and she has also been a wonderful friend to me. At three in the morning, when nothing seemed to fall into place, she would be there at the other end of the phone, offering encouragement, correcting my text, believing in me. Without Gaye, this book would never have seen the light of day. Secondly, Alan Overton has been a truly supportive friend, oiling the waters around me when it all seemed too much, believing it would all come together in the end. He also took responsibility for my company when I went bush to write, and generally made life hassle-free for me.

I would also like to thank my family and friends for putting up with me while we cooked and tasted the food for the book, and for offering their criticism and encouragement all the way through.

Ideas for recipes come from everywhere: books, classes, dining experiences and conversation. Over the years and in the heat of culinary passion many ideas have been adapted and reinterpreted into recipes I love. If I have lost trace of the origins of a dish and not acknowledged the source, I apologise.

Michael Lee-Richards

I am grateful to Agfa-Gevaert NZ Ltd for their assistance in the preparation of this book.

Johannes van Kan

FOREWORD

This book breaks the barriers. For the first time a writer lifts the lid off the emotions and personal experiences of a home cook, caterer and restaurateur.

Whether preparing a perfect romantic dinner for two or a glamorous but against-all-odds wedding for 500 in the middle of the bush, Michael shares his feelings with unbearable honesty. His love of people, entertaining and food is paramount. At last the details about freshly grated horseradish and the rarest beef cooked with a dark crust are revealed! If you think these home truths would put you off, you could be wrong. Instead you will probably be weak with sympathetic laughter and renewed with a real desire to cook.

At last we can all shamelessly share the twinges of panic familiar to all professional and home cooks, knowing that we are not alone in having the occasional mishap that we would rather not remember. And with the perennial enthusiasm that keeps us cooking, we start another day full of optimism that all will go beautifully to plan.

And it does and it shall — if you use the recipes and instructions from this book. Around each recipe you will find a wealth of helpful hints, showing that Michael has cooked each recipe dozens of times and knows its potential problems. This talented teacher carefully guides you to success. The glorious photographs are inspiring. The recipes are delicious and have brought him enormous success. All you have to do is *Cook!*

Lyn Hall

After a wide-reaching culinary career resulting in diplomas and gold medals, Lyn Hall has devoted her life to teaching and is known as the best private teacher in Europe. Her work also involves promoting the work of writers and chefs, by inviting them to teach in her cookery theatres.

speaking perso

nally

'Cooking is *never* static and *no-one* owns the recipe. Take *courage*, a good glass of wine and *cook!*'

It was fairly obvious from the start that I would have a career that would sap every ounce of my energy, for even as a child I was demanding and difficult. In the small country town where we lived I was the one who got into trouble with the neighbours, started fights and loved the sight of blood. I was always first in line for food, and ate the most.

My mother managed to feed six children imaginatively on a very limited income. She rarely used recipes, wasted nothing, and in many ways taught me a lot without my realising it. Potato scones with pea and ham soup, a fruit loaf that was just heaven — and who else in the sixties would cook the white of the silverbeet separately from the green and top it with a mustard cheese sauce? Our pantry held large jars of bottled salmon (caught by my father), jars of pickled baby carrots from the thinnings, salted beans and bottlings of every fruit we grew. Her stews may have been low in meat but every vegetable she could think of would be in there, plus herbed potato dumplings. My mother was a relaxed cook who could throw together food that had wonderful flavours, but she much preferred to be out in the garden where she was most at home.

My paternal grandmother, on the other hand, would spend hours cooking. She would cook from a recipe, adapt it to suit the ingredients she had, and produce food to die for. She would pickle eggs, hang hams until they went green, string onions, garlic and shallots, dry walnuts, and as was very common for country cooks she would preserve just about anything that lived. Her kitchen was a hive of activity. Breakfast often did not finish until 10 o'clock, and she would be straight back into cooking for the midday meal. Friends and family would eat at a large table in the middle of the room, while she would fuss around checking we all had enough. She was a cook who cooked to entertain but who took entertaining in her stride. She used the best silver, china and cutlery, whether the occasion was breakfast, lunch, dinner or a picnic. Whatever she did when it came to food, she did for comfort, style and to hell with the cost.

And so my love of food grew, from a mother who could cook wonderfully flavoured, simple food on a budget, and a grandmother who never worried about the cost as long as it had style and tasted perfect.

I remembered all this when I was first thrown into a kitchen and began to discover the whole theatre of cooking — of colour, texture and flavour. It was a revelation.

After being asked politely to leave school I went to university, studying religion, geography, sociology, criminology and law. It was fun and it was free, but what I remember best of all was my part-time job as a dishwasher at an

SPEAKING PERSONALLY

Indonesian restaurant. Over the five years I was there, I learnt the art of washing ten pots at once, of working incredibly long hours, partying late and getting to work as bright as a button the next morning for another long day. The owners were inspirational. They knew how to work, how to live and how to spend. It was a lifestyle I was not used to and I just lapped it up.

I changed city and university to complete another degree, working in another small restaurant to assist with the pennies. Again I became addicted to the life; it gave me a tremendous buzz. And again my boss was an inspiration — a powerful woman who could cook amazing food using the simplest ingredients. She encouraged me to forget about being a lawyer. Apparently I very rarely mentioned the career I had spent six years training for, and raved about food all the time. At the ripe old age of 24 I put my legal career on hold, bought a restaurant, and have never looked back.

I read Elizabeth David, cooked from Julia Child and started to study the food of the Roux brothers. I would cook for hours, learning by trial and error. I preserved, pickled and created chutneys and jams. I cooked bread that was so heavy it dented the oven trays. Often I would cook for a full house, bottle until morning, then go to the vegetable market to get the best as the sun came up.

I was young, enthusiastic and full of energy, and I believed I could do anything. So to make my life hell I bought the vegetable shop next door to the restaurant and began to learn about produce. This was a big mistake. Although I can cook into the small hours, I am not good at rising in the morning.

I learnt that I am best to stick to the job I love — I sold the vegetable shop and now leave the early morning market visits to others.

As a result of that experience I decided never to cook breakfasts, cater for early lunches, or in fact do much of anything before 11.00 a.m. I am a night person. I adore the buzz of a busy kitchen and the sounds and smells of a happy dining room. It is very satisfying to see food leave a kitchen and know that it looks and tastes great. Best of all I love that glorious feeling when I can sit down in the restaurant when all the punters have gone home, enjoy a gin and tonic that would blow your socks off, and reminisce about the evening just gone.

Once the restaurant was established we began a catering business. It was hard work, but serving 150 guests from a small domestic kitchen had its charm and managed to get the adrenaline up to a pitch that kept me satisfied. The business grew, and next thing we had separate catering premises, a manager and an expanding staff. Weddings for 200 and cocktail parties for more than a thousand became the norm. On other occasions we might cater for a small dinner party for four in the middle of a paddock, for

two on a yacht, or for 40 with silver service on an old wooden jetty at dusk. It was absorbing and satisfying, but then we had another idea. Why not give lessons in cooking?

The school was perfectly timed. A great flood of enthusiasm for new types of food was sweeping the world, and New Zealand was no exception. Wonderful chefs came from as far afield as France, England and the United States, and many popped across the Tasman to teach as well. The classes grew. The local food lovers learned more, and so did I. In addition I travelled widely, met a large number of chefs and food writers, and began to be aware of trends, of different styles and variations in use from one country to another. When I came home I was able to pass on this knowledge to others.

◆ SPEAKING PERSONALLY

I have learnt to adore bistro food, to appreciate fine French, innovative Californian, the great Italian and Mediterranean flavours and the tastes of the East untampered by western influences. I am learning about Australian seafood, about their tropical market gardens, and how climate and topography can alter the taste of a simple tomato or fresh peppercorn. I have discovered such wonders as pistachio oil, and the heady smell of white truffle oil.

When travelling I always discover something that can be used in my food. Perhaps it is a colour combination I have not thought of before, or simply a plate that would go really well with the Thai beef dish I have perfected. Perhaps it is something someone said about water chestnuts, reminding me that I haven't used them for a while; or it may be the shape of a building in San Francisco that looks so superb that I wonder if I can reproduce it in a white chocolate and almond torte. Someone might mention the glory of New Zealand scallops, and on the same day I visit an apple orchard and suddenly think: why not a green apple and scallop salad with perhaps a little Pernod and wild fennel?

Food is part of a social experience. It is wonderful to cook for people who truly enjoy your efforts, or to be served a meal that has been cooked with such care and attention to detail that you could almost murder the chef! But it can be just as good to sit down with your family over a dish of lumpy stew and mashed potatoes, if not for the food then for the enjoyment of each other's company. Cooking the best you can for people you love and enjoying their company is my idea of heaven. You cook your best when it comes from the heart.

I feel very fortunate to be a cook. I can be an artist, an interpreter and a caretaker of recipes. I can create my own combinations and present my food how I like. Who can say that I am wrong if my friends and I enjoy the finished product? I simply enjoy cooking and working with food.

I do not call myself a chef. I take nothing that seriously, and I am not professionally trained. I believe in the produce and the finished product, but I am not over-concerned about using the correct method to obtain the desired result. I have enthusiasm, I've read a lot and studied with other chefs, but mine is a trial-and-error approach. I would not insult well-trained chefs by putting myself in their bracket. To me food is a toy to be played around with, experimented with and enjoyed. I am not a finicky cook. Food should be well flavoured, simple to cook and great to eat. It needs to have colour and texture and be as light in composition as possible.

I loathe sticking to a recipe for the recipe's sake. Nothing is ever set in concrete. No one has the right to say 'this is the only way to cook'; how arrogant! I like to look at the food I have, at the freshness of the ingredients, at

'No-*one* has the *right to* say "this *is* the only *way* to cook"; how *arrogant*!'

the situation in which the food is to be served, and the guests to whom I am serving it. My friends might love a camembert, tomato and mint salad with fresh peach, for example, but some of my aunts would be horrified at such a combination. I would be better to serve them a ripe camembert with salad and fresh peaches to follow. But rest assured that if the camembert was not ripe and the brie or blue cheese was, I would change the recipe without hesitation. Why not a brie, walnut and fresh thyme salad, so long as everything is at its best and the dressing is a creation that will blow your mind.

In cooking, the basics are the most important things. A good sauce is just as crucial as the freshness of your ingredients. You need to master the art of making stock, using all the bits and pieces from around the kitchen to create a sauce of which you can be proud. When my beef stock is well flavoured, when my chicken stock tastes like good chicken stock — and not as though a sick fowl has flown over the pot — I am over the moon. If I could, I would make stock until there was no room left to store any more. From a good stock I can create magical sauces, soups and dishes in half the time it takes with all the expensive ingredients so often used. Who needs two cups of brandy in a sauce if an excellent base stock is used? Two tablespoons is more likely to be sufficient to produce a sauce that will make you weep for joy.

Just as the basics are important, so is open-mindedness. A cook or chef who knows it all should really consider changing jobs. One year, obviously before the share-market crash, I travelled around the world and attended some 30 cooking schools. I ate myself into the chubby figure I have unfortunately managed to maintain, but I also learnt an awful lot in a short time (eight weeks). Most importantly, I learnt that what is considered the only way to do something in one country is merely an alternative in another part of the world, where the results may be just as good. I tasted a superb sauce made from a can of weak watery stock in one country, then flew to another part of the world and tasted an equally wonderful sauce made from the stock of reduced bones of a farmyard spring chicken. True, the ingredients were quite different, the techniques were miles apart, but both sauces had their merits and both were right in terms of the final taste. From as simple an experience as that I had matured into a better cook. Less opinionated and miles less pig-headed!

The more experience I obtained, the more my food changed. From every chef, every book and just about every person I would learn more, and as a result I would look at my own food more closely. I would love it more or like it less, wonder what on earth I was thinking of when I created that dish and often think seriously about taking up window dressing as an alternative career.

SPEAKING PERSONALLY

My food began to lighten up, it became less complicated and the flavours became more honest. A steak was allowed to taste like a steak, and not like a paddock of garlic enriched with cream.

From such enthusiasts as Lyn Hall at La Petite Cuisine in London I learnt the importance of looking first at the true classical approach, at attention to small details and at balance in taste. From my classes at the Ritz in Paris, and especially from mixing with fellow students, I learnt the significance of various herbs and spices and the differences between them, the importance of timing in cooking, and how to incorporate new flavours into, and old flavours out of, existing favourite recipes. I also learnt that you can share six bottles of rough red wine between three people and still seriously think you can walk. From a very short meeting with a talented Auckland chef I realised that you can do what you like as long as it tastes great, sounds good on the menu, preferably is more innovative than the restaurant down the road, and doesn't have so many flavours that the result is overkill.

After reading all about Nico Ladenis and his restaurants in London, his philosophy on food and the importance he places on simplicity in a dish, from dining in his restaurants and loving the food, I began to reduce the number of ingredients I put into a dish. I began to look closely at the necessity for ingredients and the resulting combination of flavours.

This was a great learning time. In my early days in cooking I always found it easier to complicate a dish, to have sauces that were substantial, just in case the

produce was inferior, overcooked or badly cut. I would combine many different flavours to look smart and create a dish that diners would not cook for themselves at home, and probably not want to if the truth be known. I covered my lack of knowledge with bulk flavour, cream and sauces so thick you could walk on them. As my knowledge developed my skill improved, and my love of good honest flavours began to evolve. My dishes became lighter and I realised that the ability to create a simple dish perfectly is harder than it looks.

I looked at the use of juices, vinaigrettes, infused oils and vegetable broths and where I could I took out the thick creamy sauces and the heavily reduced stocks which can be so rich and overpowering — despite the fact that I still love a sauce that is creamy, filling and wicked for my ever-constant diet.

From reading the works of Alice Waters of Chez Panisse in San Francisco and from enjoying her food I became aware of the importance of the freshness of produce, the use of organically grown vegetables, and the move away from additives in food and chemicals in rearing animals. The difference between a stock made from battery chickens and a stock made from free-range chickens is not only that a battery-chicken stock is often cloudy due to their diet, but it lacks real flavour.

Fresh herbs have become even more important to me. We have planters in both the catering and restaurant kitchens, and small pots of various herbs are on show at most classes in the school. I employed a gardener to put in a herb patch at the house and planted fruit trees, walnut and hazelnut trees, grapevines, mulberry and fig trees. I conned my family into supplying green garlic for sauces, lemon balm and nasturtium flowers for salads, wild strawberries, lavender, bronze fennel and even dandelion; black violets for garnish, blackcurrant leaves for making a great sorbet, and plump overripe black grapes for a black grape and cardamom ice cream. Home suppliers drop off wonderfully fresh gooseberries, vine-ripened yellow tomatoes, fennel bulbs and baby basil leaves. Whereas once upon a time I would have been more concerned with the sauce, the accompaniment, and the ease of cooking, now I concentrate on the quality of the initial produce. A top-quality ingredient cooked simply, with restraint used in the accompaniments and presentation, is a wonderful thing.

One of my greatest pleasures is to hand on all the ideas, the recipes and the latest food fads that I collect from around the world. Each week we have a meeting for the staff of each kitchen where we discuss new ideas. When cooking we discuss recipes and chop and change them to keep them right up to date, and we have small classes just for staff once a month where we test

◦ SPEAKING PERSONALLY

new ideas and taste new flavours. This is an essential part of working as a team, especially when, as in our case, there is so much going on. Not only are there the staff who operate the restaurant and the catering company, but others work solely on television work, assist with recipe research for magazines, operate the hire company, the food-manufacturing side of the business — and there are separate staff again whose job it is to make sure I don't forget to take my recipes to a class.

As part of this sharing process, as well as to fund my numerous trips, improve my knowledge and give me an entrée into some of the best schools, and the opportunity to meet some of the most accomplished food writers, chefs and teachers, I began to teach at other cooking schools. It was gruelling to teach and entertain at the same time, but with the help of a little claret I got through. To demonstrate in your own kitchen is simple in comparison. To get up at four in the morning, pack up everything from whisks to beaters, half-prepped dishes and half-awake staff, and fly off to teach in a kitchen you haven't been in before is not good for the nerves. We have found ourselves miles from home, realised we have forgotten to pack the recipes and left the knives on the footpath, then been told that we will of course feed the farmhand, the eight shearers and the four children. Fortunately my parents objected to swearing, and with luck no one heard what was said to the staff out in the pantry, but the air definitely had a blue tinge on that occasion.

We have taught classes in private schools, art galleries, church halls and department stores, unused warehouses, ex-railway stations and farmhouses. But of all the classes we have held over the last few years the most rewarding was teaching the inmates of a prison. They expected nothing but knowledge and loved every minute of it, asking questions about the food, the chemistry of the recipe, and cooking as a career. We were all blown away by how much we were appreciated.

One of the first classes I attended abroad was with a very talented chef who drank quite a lot as he taught. This is it, I thought, and promptly wrote myself off in the next class I was teaching. I have fallen over, dropped dishes, combined the wrong ingredients and cut great gashes out of my fingers as I worked (and unfortunately that was in a vegetarian class). I have flooded sinks, set fire to tea towels and sprayed the students in the front row with mayonnaise, oversalted, underseasoned, banged my head on badly placed shelves and said words to make your skin crawl. Yet still the classes have filled, the students have been appreciative, and we can still afford to travel.

From those who attend my classes I have acquired a pool of food lovers on my team. People who love to cook, who will try new combinations and review old ones, and people who will laugh at a disaster and carry it all off with style. I have found friends among my students who think a lot like I do with regard to food, who enjoy elegant French, classy American or simple homely food, who will cook to all hours, fall asleep with cookbooks and dream about food. Some are professional chefs and writers, others are shopkeepers and teachers, but they all leave little tags in their books for recipes to be tried, they all have food stains on the pages, and they would all walk on glass to get the very best asparagus of the season, the best butter available and the most suitable wine for their meal.

From teaching in cooking schools, the next progression was to television; again, following a few entertaining disasters, it has all fallen into place. Just local television, but what a great place to learn. To burst into laughter in front of Canterbury as the oven door falls off is one thing, but to do it in front of national television is definitely the sort of thing to keep you awake at night. To see a stunning smoked oyster soufflé rise to great heights in the oven, look excellent as you carry it gently out and promptly drop it, is not 'a good look'. But to see the face of the presenter as you blow-torch a sabayon, as you let his delicate nose smell raclette for the  first time, or as you introduce him to Thelma, your favourite kitchen blender, is worth every minute.

To teach cooking has become one of the true joys of my life, whether it is to staff at the restaurant or catering company, at the school or on television, in the magazines I write for, or simply trying to tell someone not to boil cabbage for two hours. It is one of the most rewarding aspects of food, along with cooking in the restaurant, the photography styling, the catering, and of course the travel.

I try to get away at least four times a year, and more if the budget will handle it. The excitement of planning a trip, organising schools to teach at or be taught by, restaurants to dine in and with any luck to assist in for a night or two, is great. The new ideas, the recipes you see and the flavours that you experience are simply magical. Without this constant kick in the pants of my recipe collection I would become very stale.

It is without doubt invaluable to read, to cook and to study food constantly if you are to stay in the game, but the experience of seeing all these great chefs in

◆ SPEAKING PERSONALLY

action, to sit at a table with one of your mentors and actually to talk to such greats as Julia Child, Alice Waters, Michel Roux, Lyn Hall, Di Holuigue and Joanne Weir is beyond belief.

In tandem with all the new ideas, the new recipes and the changes in approach to food, it is in fact the change in the public's attitude towards their eating habits that has had the greatest effect on the way chefs cook: the change to less salt, cream, eggs and red meat, and more fish and white meat, fresh vegetables, herbs and pasta. Twelve years ago béchamel sauce, with its cream and milk, its good hearty flavours and thick consistency, was very popular in restaurants; today it is rarely seen. We have 'trim milk', 'lite cream' and numerous other weight-watchers' wonders that assist cooks in their constant endeavour to provide what the customer wants.

While people dine out much more than they ever used to, they are aware of their cholesterol levels, their weight, and how they will look at their next gym work-out. They are more health-conscious than ever before, and if they are to dine in your restaurant more than once a year the food must reflect that. We have become more of a 'grazing' public, more inclined to have a light meal rather than four courses, more inclined to drink mineral water (sparkling, of course), and the wine we now enjoy with our meal is most likely to be light and dry.

We are educated eaters who discuss and analyse food, and dine around to get variety. We like good service, properly housed wines and comfortable surroundings, and to make it hard on ourselves, we like to entertain at home. As a result of all this growing knowledge we need to be as good as the last restaurant we criticised, as organised as a caterer and as thoughtful as the concierge at a top hotel. Without good, well-trained staff a miracle is needed, or perhaps a good well-organised book to guide you, one that offers recipes that won't let you down, and gives alternatives if you find you are out of a particular ingredient.   ◆

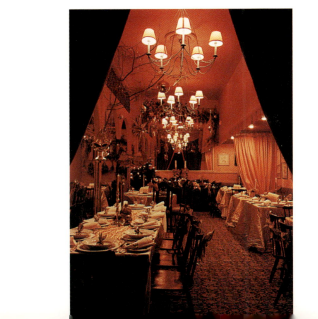

fabulous finger

food

Avocado Blini with Whitebait	24
Bean Salsa	25
Little Camembert Eclairs with Walnut Butter	26
Chicken Almondine	28
Peach Chutney	29
Little Tartlets of Field Mushroom Risotto with White Truffle Oil	30
White Wine and Cheese Fritters	32
Minted Lamb Tartlets with Soft Parmesan Crust	33
Tabil	33
Tartare of New Zealand Venison	34
Chilli Spiced Almonds with Cumin	36
Roulade of Saffron with Double-Cream Brie	38
Homemade Saffron Ricotta	39
Grilled Raddichio with Chilli Beef	40

*O*ne of the most pleasant ways to entertain is with hors d'oeuvres, finger food or canapés. Whatever term you prefer, it is in reality, to quote one of my clients, 'food on the hoof'. It is superb for an elegant cocktail party, a thank-you to a fellow worker, or a sunrise bash for the shearers who have finished the job well in budget. Finger-food functions can have as much style as you wish, be directed totally by the guests and the occasion, or simply be a pre-dinner nibble before a great evening of dining and theatre.

This is a perfect way to feed a large number of guests with little effort, little space and the least hassle of all. The food should be well flavoured, small — one mouthful in size — and interesting. Sure, you can serve trays of nicely chilled little yellow tomatoes, white radishes and fresh strawberries, but you also need one or two items that will fascinate your guests and push their tastebuds to the limit.

If your party begins at six your guests will not have eaten, so be prompt, and have some substantial food to absorb the first glass of wine. If finger food is to be offered throughout the evening have a wide variety, with light crisp food at the start, a little more substance as you move towards the middle of the evening, and perhaps something magical and sweet as you come towards the end of the function.

We have held cocktail parties on yachts, trains and riversides, in glasshouses, great halls and paddocks. We have used orchards, woolsheds and country airfields, and we have incorporated finger food into theatre shows, large christenings, weddings and company launches. We have organised and catered for 1930s cocktail parties, ship launches, art exhibitions, ski parties and deer sales. We have catered for the wealthy, the stylish and the theatrical, as well as the less affluent, and even criminals. Every function is different in style, in content and in budget, but every one has been a success.

This is one of the most versatile forms of entertaining, and one of the most exciting for guests, waiting staff and chefs. For a small cocktail party of up to about fifty most of the work is done on the day, with one chef and one pantry hand; for up to a thousand guests it takes two chefs and three pantry staff, and three days of good hard work; for larger parties we just work on up. We have catered for four thousand in seven marquees, a mammoth effort that stretched all the staff to their limits, but we managed despite the electricity blowing, the ovens overheating and the coffee not arriving until the very last moment. We have had a formal cocktail party with a bike shed as the kitchen, a finger-food wedding where the laundry was the only space we could work from, and a

◦ FABULOUS FINGER FOOD

book launch where the guest of honour was so drunk we were looking after him more than the guests. Very few functions run exactly as planned, but with a smile, a swift change when necessary and a hushed voice, no one would notice.

On one occasion we catered for seven hundred out of a woolshed in the middle of a small forest. The shed had just been cleaned out by the farmhands the night before so the place was clean and tidy, but very busy with mice trying to find a new home. Two of my chefs would not work inside the shed, setting up trestles outside the back door despite the cold and drizzle. One of my pantry staff was more on top of the table than working with the food, always sure she heard something, and when we threw two little brie and almond muffins along the floor towards the staff the room was vacated in 1.5 seconds flat. Every job has its perks and that was one of my finer moments. ◦

Avocado Blini *with* Whitebait

2 eggs, lightly beaten
⅔ cup flour
½ teaspoon salt
3–4 tablespoons milk
pulp of 1 ripe avocado
200 g (7 oz) drained whitebait
zest of 1 lemon
1 teaspoon cracked white pepper
3 tablespoons butter
2 tablespoons olive oil

This recipe evolved as a result of a client saying she loved avocados and could we come up with something a little unusual. We played around with the idea for some time and came up with this avocado blini. Although not a true blini, it is very similar in texture if eaten immediately after cooking. Sometimes we may add a little baking powder to lighten the mixture, or fold in some egg white to give it a creamy texture. It is such a good recipe that we have used it repeatedly over the last five years, with numerous variations. The blini are cooked in butter and oil combined, on a high heat, so that they are crisp on the outside but still soft and runny like guacamole on the inside. You can either include the whitebait in the batter, as we have here, or omit it from the batter and pile it on top.

Method

Combine the eggs, flour, salt, milk and avocado in a processor and work until smooth. The mixture should lean more towards a thick batter, but more milk may be needed if it is too thick to mix, or a little extra flour if it is too liquid. The texture will vary a tad with the size of the avocado. Fold in the whitebait, lemon and pepper just before cooking.

Heat a frypan or grilling plate and pour on a little of the butter and oil. Put small spoonfuls of batter onto the pan and cook over a medium-high heat for a minute on each side, or until golden brown. The blini will still be moist within, rather like guacamole with a crust. Repeat until you have cooked all the batter.

Notes

We usually serve the blini topped with crème fraîche and angle-sliced chives. If you prefer, you can sauté the whitebait separately, mix it with sour cream or crème fraîche and pile it on top. However, folding the uncooked whitebait through the mixture prior to cooking is an easy way to reduce last-minute work.

You can serve these as a small sandwich, which makes them easy to pick up and eat. For this we pipe red pepper or smoked bacon mousse between two blini and serve them piled up on large silver trays. They make a wonderful talking point at a cocktail party.

The easiest way to remove the flesh from an avocado is to run a knife around the fruit, twist it and split the two halves. Tap the seed firmly with a sharp knife and it will come out with the knife. Run a dessertspoon around the skin and the flesh will come out easily. If the avocado is not quite ripe add a pinch of icing sugar to the recipe. As with anything green, I find white pepper is great for lifting flavour.

For a plated appetiser, an entrée or perhaps a light luncheon dish, keep the whitebait separate and make the avocado blini slightly larger than usual. Layer three blini, club-sandwich style with the whitebait as the filling, and serve with yellow pepper coulis (page 135). The combination is colourful, well-flavoured and definitely unusual.

Avocado blini topped with crème fraîche, smoked salmon and caviar is an elegant canapé and one we often serve at very smart functions. Check that the smoked salmon is not too salty, as combined with the caviar it can be a blow-out saltwise if you are not careful.

Leftover blini can be reheated the next day and served crisp, with a dipping bowl of avocado mayonnaise.

Always cook one blini first and check the seasoning. Remember these may be served while guests are drinking, so do season them well.

Use pumpkin instead of avocado and add fresh nutmeg. Serve with aïoli or rémoulade. We sometimes serve these with a bean salsa.

Bean *Salsa*

There are lots of recipes for Bean Salsa but this is one of our favourites.

Method

Combine all the ingredients in a food processor until they have emulsified, retaining some texture. Season to taste with salt and pepper. Should you wish to lift the flavour of this salsa more, add a splash of french dressing.

60 g (2 oz) parsley
3 spring onions, finely chopped
1 garlic clove, peeled
60 ml (2 fl oz) extra virgin olive oil
90 ml (3 fl oz) mild peanut oil
2 red chillies, finely chopped
2 tablespoons lemon juice
zest of 2 lemons
½ cup cooked, drained
red kidney beans

Little Camembert Eclairs *with* Walnut Butter

450 ml (¾ pint) water
180 g (6 oz) butter, diced
250 g (8 oz) flour, sieved
½ teaspoon sea salt
½ teaspoon freshly grated nutmeg
½ teaspoon freshly ground white pepper
1 small camembert, frozen and grated
5 eggs, lightly beaten

One of the most versatile recipes for a caterer is choux pastry. I must have made thousands of these little éclairs. We refer to them with affection as 'slugs', largely because of their shape and size, and also to differentiate them from what are called 'the little puffs'. The choice of what you can create with these is limitless, but if you are to have a wonderful filling it is important to lift the flavour by using a complementary seasoning in the choux. Nutmeg in this pastry is wonderful, or you could add some finely chopped walnut, or just season it with extra white pepper.

If you intend to store walnuts for some time it is best to keep them in the freezer, taking out what you need as you go. This will stop them going rancid and ruining a dish. In Christchurch we are very fortunate in having excellent walnut groves nearby, and as a result we buy them in once a year, shell them and freeze them straight away. Fresh walnuts are, of course, always best.

Method

Preheat the oven to 200°C/400°F. Put the water and butter into a saucepan over low heat and gently melt the butter. When the butter is dissolved bring it to the boil and throw in the sieved flour, salt, nutmeg and white pepper, beating vigorously for about a minute. Cook for a further 2 minutes, stirring gently so the batter does not catch on the bottom of the pan. Remove from the heat, add the grated cheese and leave to cool. Put into a food processor and slowly beat in the lightly beaten eggs. The pastry is ready to use as soon as all the eggs are incorporated.

Pipe 2 cm (1 in) strips onto damp oven trays, leaving a gap between each to allow for expansion during cooking. You may wish to spray the éclairs with water before putting them into the oven as the steam helps with the rising.

Once the éclairs are cooked and lightly golden, about 12 minutes, remove them from the oven and split them to let the steam out. Fill with a spoonful of walnut butter, pile up on silver trays and serve.

Walnut Butter

Chop the shallots finely, heat a small pan and sauté with the butter until lightly coloured. Put into a food processor with all the other ingredients and pulse until amalgamated. Check the seasoning and spoon into the small choux cases. Adding a thin slice of avocado at this stage creates a delicious colour and taste sensation.

6 shallots
60 g (2 oz) butter
250 g (8 oz) walnuts
90 g (3 oz) soft camembert
½ cup fresh white breadcrumbs
15 g (½ oz) butter
salt, pepper and cayenne to taste
avocado (optional)

Notes

When making choux pastry always make sure the water does not boil before the butter is melted. This is a common mistake which results in a very oily panade (mixture).

The colour of éclairs is not particularly exciting and the last thing you want at a cocktail party is a wave of beige, so when filling the éclairs be generous and have some colour showing, place them on brightly coloured trays and use herbs to decorate them.

Like most pastry, it is always best to make the éclairs up on the day they are needed. However, if necessary they can be made up and frozen in airtight containers. Refresh these from frozen in a warming drawer or a very low temperature oven. When cooked and not used, éclairs can be processed to make superb crumbs for another dish.

Some combinations we find great for cocktail parties

Smoked oyster and mushroom éclairs served on large red lacquered trays lined with herbs.

Chicken and brandied apricot éclairs with celery, piled up on trays lined with white linen and dusted with celery seeds.

Orange éclairs with smoked duck salad served on large silver trays with a sprinkling of orange zest and cracked black pepper.

Thyme-enriched éclairs with a salad of rare lamb, julienne of red pepper and black olives; these we serve piled on scrubbed wooden chopping boards.

Horseradish éclairs with roast beef and pickled walnuts; a finger food that looks superb on the old blue and white meat platters.

At one of our more off-beat weddings we served as a wedding cake a tower of lemon choux puffs filled with a smoked salmon mousse, and walnut éclairs filled with a mushroom, apple and Cognac pâté. It was presented as a savoury wedding cake with fresh herbs, nasturtium flowers and young grapevine leaves tucked in. The bridal couple served it to the guests in the traditional style of a croquembouche. This was at a finger-food wedding for three hundred. To achieve the size and drama needed for this we had a special metal frame made to accommodate six hundred miniature puffs. Since then we have used the same idea to provide a surprise at finger-food functions, with two waiters carrying the tower around for guests just to help themselves from. At a fireworks party for a large corporate function we went to the extreme of having sparklers lit on the tower as staff moved among the guests.

Chicken Almondine

This recipe is an illustration of the versatility of choux pastry, and is perfect for catering for large numbers. Choux pastry that is flavoured and deep-fried is often referred to as a 'beignet'. In this case the choux pastry has everything folded in while it is still warm and it is then deep-fried or baked.

This is one of my favourites recipes. It was created from the need to use up cooked chicken and provide greater variety for a large gathering. Without the chicken this is a great recipe for vegetarians as it is still well flavoured and has good texture.

Method

Put the water and butter into a saucepan over low heat and gently melt the butter. When dissolved bring to a boil and throw in the sieved flour; beat vigorously for

450 ml (¾ pint) water
180 g (6 oz) butter, diced
250 g (8 oz) flour, sieved
5 eggs, lightly beaten
3 egg whites
1 cup finely chopped cooked chicken meat
60 g (2 oz) chopped blanched almonds
zest from 2 oranges
1 teaspoon each ground ginger, cinnamon and cardamom
½ teaspoon each freshly ground nutmeg, garlic paste and finely chopped chives
1 teaspoon salt
1 teaspoon Dijon mustard
1 teaspoon chilli sauce
½ teaspoon Worcestershire sauce
1 teaspoon freshly ground white pepper
oil to deep-fry

FABULOUS FINGER FOOD

about a minute. Cook for a further two minutes, stirring gently so that the batter does not catch on the bottom of the pan. Remove from the heat and leave to cool. Put into a food processor and slowly beat in the lightly beaten eggs. Beat the egg whites until stiff and put to one side. Add all the remaining ingredients to the choux pastry, fold in the egg whites to loosen the mixture and put all to one side while the oil is heating up to 180°C/350°F.

Deep-fry spoonfuls, until golden and crisp. Drain thoroughly. Serve hot and crisp, with your favourite pickle or sauce. We love to serve these with peach chutney.

Peach Chutney

Skin, stone and slice the peaches. Heat the peaches with the other ingredients, bringing the mixture slowly to the boil, stirring gently, until the sugar is dissolved. Boil gently for 5 minutes. Ladle into warm jars and seal. Use after 1 week.

500 g (1 lb) peaches
1½ cups cider vinegar
1 tablespoon fresh ginger, minced
1 tablespoon ground coriander
3 cloves garlic
1½ teaspoons tamarind paste (or the juice and rind of 1 lemon)
½ cup sugar
¼ teaspoon chilli powder
¼ teaspoon finely ground black pepper

Notes

Fresh oysters and bacon make a great beignet. Use the liquid from the oysters in the water of the choux pastry, dry the oysters well and pre-grill the bacon. This will reduce the risk of the beignets splattering when they are deep-fried. Season well and serve piled on large trays with lemon. Scallops are also excellent done this way and go very well with green apple.

To reheat beignets or little choux éclairs we put them into a roasting dish, cover them with a damp towel and gently heat them in a low oven. The steam from the towel will revive the choux pastry.

Fresh or smoked salmon beignets are wonderful, even more so if lime and ginger are added to the flavourings.

Fold into your choux grated tasty cheese, coarsely diced mozzarella, mustard and a generous pinch of nutmeg and you have a cheese beignet that goes well with a tart plum chutney, the peach chutney or a fresh apple salsa.

Roasted garlic beignets are a delight to serve as tiny finger food piled into napkin-lined bowls, as an accompaniment to a beef main course or floating in a soup of field mushrooms and red wine.

Roasted tomato and eggplant beignets, served with pesto that has been thinned down with a little oil, are very well received, as are caramelised onion beignets with a sauce made from Kapiti double-blue cheese.

If, when adding an ingredient to choux pastry, the choux becomes too wet, fold in soft white breadcrumbs. The seasoning may need to be adjusted but at least the mixture will not separate or splatter when it is deep-fried. An alternative is to put spoonfuls into mini muffin tins and bake.

Little Tartlets *of* Field Mushroom Risotto *with* White Truffle Oil

This recipe evolved just after I had completed the most exciting course with Lyn Hall of La Petite Cuisine at Waterside Inn, which is at Bray, just out of London. There were only three other students: Joan Walker, a most inspirational woman who mails me a regular supply of new recipes and ideas that she collects and uses when entertaining either on her boat on the Thames, at her home 'Cottons' in Kent, or at her holiday home in Florida; John Dove, who is chef to the Oppenheimer family in South Africa; and Mark Webb, a talented caterer and chef. From that class alone I have made great friends, extended my recipe library via airmail, and had assistance via fax with several difficult functions.

Just after I had returned from the London trip an aunt of mine who was farming at the time dropped in a large supply of the most heady smelling mushrooms. It seemed a waste to freeze them as they were just perfect. I looked at the recipes we had cooked at Bray and adapted one to serve as finger food at a function we had for the then Governor-General. It was a great success. With pastry for the little tartlet cases put through the pasta machine to get it extra thin, the finished product made me proud.

I once cooked this recipe as part of an exam at a cooking school in the United States. The others in the class were health conscious to the extreme in what they did and did not eat. It was a most boring class. So not only did I add the butter and parmesan according to the recipe, I added another 300 grams of butter right at the end, extra white wine and some more parmesan. I had cooked enough for eight, there were four tutors tasting and not a piece of rice was left over. Of course it was New Zealand butter, and the wine was a good New Zealand white, but I do believe if they knew they had scoffed down about 1000 calories per serve they would have died on the spot. I passed the course with flying colours and I'm sure it had a lot to do with this wonderful dish. By the way, it does not require that extra butter unless you are feeding some very tiresome dieters.

White truffle oil is not always available, it is not cheap and it will go rancid if not kept chilled. It is, however, one of the few ingredients I wouldn't be without (a product

✥ FABULOUS FINGER FOOD

introduced to me by Lyn Hall). Only a few drops are needed to lift the flavour of the mushrooms into a different dimension, to make what is a great dish sublime. Walnut, pistachio or hazelnut oil will do, or you could omit the extra oil totally.

This recipe can be served as a first or a main course, and as it is one of my personal favourites I often reheat it for supper — it's just perfect with a gin and tonic, a little Mozart and time to browse through your favourite cookbooks, again.

Method

2 l (4 pints) mushroom stock (see Basics)
30 ml (2 tablespoons) olive oil
6 shallots, finely diced
250 g (8 oz) coarsely chopped dark field mushrooms
250 g (8 oz) Arborio, Vialone Nano or Carnaroli rice
150 ml (5 fl oz) white wine
60 g (2 oz) butter
60 g (2 oz) parmesan, freshly grated
white truffle oil to taste
sea salt and freshly grated white pepper
tartlet cases (see Basics)

Place the stock in a saucepan and bring it to a simmer.

Heat the olive oil in a wide pan and cook the shallots over a low heat until they are soft and golden. Add half the mushrooms and the rice and stir to coat well with the oil. Stir for about 5 minutes. Turn the heat up to medium and add a quarter of the hot stock, keeping the rice mixture simmering and stirring constantly. When the stock is absorbed add another cup. Repeat this procedure until all the stock is absorbed and the rice is tender (about 30 minutes), reserving 3 or 4 tablespoons of stock to add later. Add the remaining mushrooms and cook for another minute. Remove the pan from the heat, and stop the cooking by adding the wine. Vigorously stir in the butter, parmesan and a generous splash of white truffle oil. Check for final seasoning then add the reserved stock, or water if you have used all the stock, to give it a rich silkiness.

The finished texture of the rice should be fully cooked, but still firm towards the centre of each grain. The risotto should be moist but not runny, so that when you put a spoonful into the tartlet case it holds its shape with perhaps just the slightest suggestion of movement. I cook this in quite large quantities and fill the tartlet cases while they are still warm. This avoids the problem of the pastry going soft, and maximises the effect of the creamy risotto, with its tantalising smell of truffles. The mixture will easily fill 4 dozen tartlet cases, leaving some to store for later use.

Notes

Carnaroli and Vialone Nano rice are both grown just out of Verona, in Italy, by the Ferron family. The Vialone Nano is a 'semi fino' rice, which has a stubby small grain. It has a delicate, almost earthy flavour, and a great capacity to absorb liquid, almost twice its own weight. Carnaroli is classified as 'super fino' because it has a larger and longer grain. It is slightly nutty in flavour and absorbs less liquid, approximately one and a half times its own grain weight. Carnaroli rice produces a drier risotto that is slightly more 'al dente' in texture.

Arborio rice is the most commonly known risotto rice grown commercially in Italy.

Notes

Glaze the inside of the pastry cases with lightly beaten egg white as soon as they come out of the oven; this will help prevent the cases going soft when they are filled. This trick is often used inside fruit flans to prevent the soggy bottom problem.

Leftover risotto can be made into fritters. Fold through a few lightly beaten egg whites, drop a tablespoon of the mixture into 1 cm (½ in) of hot oil and cook until crisp. Alternatively put the risotto in a mould and finish it off in the oven with a sprinkling of parmesan for a crust. Check the flavour of the risotto as it may need more seasoning, and you might like to add finely chopped water chestnuts or celery to give it a crunchier texture.

The stock used for risotto is important. If you are making a pumpkin risotto, the juice from cooking the pumpkin should be used instead of, or as well as, the stock. A scallop risotto would be made using lightly flavoured scallop or fish stock, and of course add the scallops just before you are ready to serve; they will cook with the heat of the rice. If the stock is too strongly flavoured it will become overpowering and sticky as it cooks and reduces, damaging the light flavour of the shellfish.

White Wine *and* Cheese Fritters

I was taught this recipe by a Swiss family I stayed with in New York. It is rich, moist and crisp all at the same time, and was often served just before dinner with a glass of sparkling red wine.

I played around with the recipe to find the best New Zealand cheese to use, and settled on Canterbury Red because of its mild flavour and its colour. Edam or mild tasty would do just as well, but will not have the colour. Practise with your favourite cheese and see what happens. But have faith — when I first tried this recipe I never thought it would work. I could see the cheese slowly melting and spreading across the hot oil in one big mess. But it does work, and it is stunning.

Method

Heat the oil to 180°C/350°F in a large pot.

Combine the finely grated cheese with the flour, eggs, garlic, spices, white wine and Kirsch. Mix to a smooth paste and, using a small spatula or knife, spread on the bread circles, forming a dome in the middle (a melon baller works wonderfully for this). Put to one side to chill and firm up.

Drop in small batches into the hot oil and turn with a pair of tongs to make sure both sides are golden. Drain on paper towels and serve.

750 g (25 oz) Canterbury Red cheese, or gruyère, finely grated
45 g (1½ oz) flour, sieved
2 eggs, lightly beaten
1 clove garlic, finely chopped
¼ teaspoon cayenne pepper
¼ teaspoon nutmeg
splash of white wine
splash of Kirsch (optional)
8 slices white bread, cut into rounds 2 cm (1 in) in diameter with a cookie cutter
2 cups oil for deep-frying

Notes

These are small in size but deceptively rich, so do not serve them as canapes for cocktails that may only last a short time before a grand four-course meal. Serve them as more substantial finger food when the function is to continue into the evening, as an accompaniment to a winter soup, just one or two before dinner, or perhaps as an evening snack to go with mulled wine after a day's skiing.

The fritters can be made up and chilled for a day or two before cooking but once cooked I prefer not to hold them for more than a few hours. Serve accompanied by spiced salts, a balsamic vinegar, a Dijon mustard mayonnaise or slices of crisp green apple.

Make larger fritters, using a cup as the template for the base, and serve one per person on salad greens with apple aïoli, pickled pear or perhaps some pickled watermelon rind.

FABULOUS FINGER FOOD

Minted Lamb Tartlets *with* Soft Parmesan Crust

3 shallots, finely chopped
1 tablespoon oil
½ teaspoon paprika
1½ teaspoons tabil (see below)
salt and cracked black pepper
250 g (8 oz) good lean lamb, very finely diced
3–4 tomatoes, peeled, seeded and diced
1½ tablespoons mint, finely chopped
¼ cup grated parmesan
1 tablespoon breadcrumbs, fresh or dried
4 eggs, lightly beaten
tartlet cases (see Basics)

I love Moroccan flavours and this little canapé was designed from the ingredients used in a lamb tajine. I created it for a cocktail party I was catering for at a friend's art gallery in San Francisco. The barely cooked lamb, so sweet and moist, the flavours of tabil, fresh mint and parmesan, and the crispness of the little tartlet cases make a most pleasant pre-dinner nibble. Once again New Zealand lamb was a resounding success. The Californians love parmesan, I love tabil, and in this combination with such a light meat, how could anyone possibly fail?

An important point with this dish is that the lamb is cooked over very high heat, very quickly — it should only take a few minutes in the pan. On no account should the lamb be cooked so that the liquid is running clear. The meat base is put into the little cases, the parmesan crust put on top, and this is slid into the oven for barely long enough to set the crust and warm the canapé. Serve these straight from the oven and make more than you think necessary. I always find that these get eaten so fast I can barely keep up the supply.

Method

Preheat the oven to 180°C/350°F. In a very hot pan, sauté the shallots in the oil with the paprika, tabil and some cracked black pepper. Once coloured, add the lamb and cook rare. Add the tomato and remove from the heat. Salt lightly.

In a separate bowl combine the mint, parmesan, breadcrumbs and eggs, and mix well.

Place the warm lamb into little pastry cases, hollowed-out tomatoes, or mini ramekins. Top with the egg mixture and put into the oven for 2 minutes exactly. The top must barely be cooked and these should be served just hot.

Tabil

Combine all the ingredients in a small spice grinder and mix to a fine powder. At the restaurant we use an electric coffee grinder solely for spices, but you can of course use a mortar and pestle; grind as finely as possible. An electric coffee grinder is a good investment but be very careful not to use your spice grinder for coffee or you will have coffee with a most wicked taste.

1 tablespoon coriander seeds
1½ teaspoons caraway seeds
2 cloves garlic, finely chopped
1 teaspoon dried chillies, crushed

Tartare *of* New Zealand Venison

I simply adore the flavour of raw meat, although I must confess my opinion changed while I was up on the farm writing this book. One of the young deer was out in the paddock limping and I had to stop myself rushing out with a bucket of warm water, some bandages and two aspirin. I am going to review this attitude to meat as soon as I have sorted out how a good full-bodied red wine goes with lentil salad.

Method

If the capers are salted rinse them several times in fresh water before chopping them finely. Place the capers, onion or shallots, spring onions, red pepper, gherkins and parsley in a bowl. Put the meat, egg yolks and pepper in a separate bowl and keep this, the finely chopped vegetables and the dressing separate until 30 minutes before serving, otherwise the vinegar from the pickles and the dressing will start to cook the meat and give you a grey tartare, rather than one that glistens. When ready, combine all, check the seasoning and serve. I find some French dressings quite sharp and often add a pinch of sugar to mellow the tartare.

Notes

Any meat can be used for this dish, but the venison is perfect as it has no fat. With beef use the best, with lamb use the tenderloin, and whatever meat you choose remove all blue skin and fat.

Serve the tartare in little cocktail tomatoes, in mini pastry cases, hollowed out cucumber cases, wrapped in nori, or simply in a chilled silver bowl with accompanying bowls of diced gherkins, small capers, rock salt and lightly cooked quails' eggs. Provide some fresh toast fingers to eat it with, and let guests help themselves.

Raw meat is not recommended for pregnant women so either avoid this dish totally or fry yourself a pattie and create an upmarket burger. The flavour is so good it would be a shame to miss out.

1 tablespoon capers, finely chopped
1 medium red onion or 6 shallots, finely chopped
3 spring onions, finely chopped
½ cup pickled red pepper, finely chopped
3 gherkins, finely chopped
½ cup finely chopped parsley
250 g (8 oz) finely diced venison fillet
2 egg yolks
generous grind of black pepper
3 tablespoons French dressing (see Basics)

FABULOUS FINGER FOOD

'To *burst* into laughter in front of *Canterbury* as the oven door falls off is one thing, but to do it in front of national television is *definitely* the sort of thing to keep you *awake* at night.'

Chilli-Spiced Almonds *with* Cumin

I have always served these at Christmas. They were a favourite of my maternal grandmother and we have all carried on the tradition of having large bowls of them available for unexpected guests. My younger sister, who believes that cumin smells like an animal that died three weeks ago in a humid temperature, prefers to use nutmeg. The flavour is nothing like the original, but she's happy. Always make more of these than you think necessary as everyone will love them.

Method

3 tablespoons peanut oil
350 g (12 oz) whole blanched almonds
125 g (4 oz) sugar
1½ teaspoons salt
1½ teaspoons ground cumin
1 teaspoon hot chilli pepper flakes
1 small fresh chilli, finely chopped
1 tablespoon sugar

Heat the oil in a heavy-bottomed frying pan over medium-high heat. Add the almonds and sprinkle the 125 g (4 oz) sugar over them. Sauté until the almonds become golden brown and stir until the sugar caramelises. Remove the almonds from the pan and toss them in a bowl with the salt, cumin, pepper flakes, fresh chilli and the remaining sugar. Tip onto an oiled baking sheet to cool, and break into pieces. Serve warm or at room temperature. Store in an airtight tin.

Walnuts and pecans can be treated in the same way, with excellent results; also try cooked chickpeas or pumpkin seeds.

Spiced Almonds

¼ cup sugar
1 tablespoon cinnamon
pinch of salt
1 egg white, unbeaten
180 g (6 oz) almonds, blanched

Preheat the oven to 180°C/350°F. In a small bowl combine the sugar, cinnamon and salt, add the egg white, and mix well. Stir in the almonds and spread onto an oven tray. Leave for 15 minutes to dry slightly, then bake in the oven until toasted and crisp — about 12 minutes, but check regularly as ovens do vary. Cool and store in an airtight container.

◆ FABULOUS FINGER FOOD

Notes

When working with hot sugar be very well organised, have all your ingredients at hand, have a bowl of cold water beside you in case you should come into contact with the hot mixture, and have a well-oiled heat-resistant tray ready to pour the almonds onto.

If you like the flavour of chilli, leave the small seeds in the chilli when chopping it.

These make excellent Christmas presents; simply put them into decorative airtight glass jars and finish with a large tartan bow. The spiced almonds prepared by my day chef Ann are an equally good alternative. Ann is a talented cook, looks after me like a sister, and always double checks the flavours in my sauces to see that I haven't gone overboard. A Cordon Bleu-style chef, Ann has always pushed the principle of less is better. She introduced me to classical cooking in my early days, and over the last fifteen years has been by my side to guide and argue with me. She has hidden my mistakes from other chefs, helped me understand seasonings, and taught me that if you do not understand what a good roast, gravy or custard is, there is no way you can understand meat cooking, making a demi-glace or cooking egg sauces. She is a real cook right down to her size six shoes, and like many good cooks she is an expert gardener, supplying the restaurant with many of its herbs and offbeat lettuces.

Roulade *of* Saffron *with* Double-Cream Brie

What people see in these upmarket omelettes I will never know — if I see another spinach roulade I will be ill. They're done to death at every function you go to, sliced so thinly that you get no flavour, and almost always filled with yet another bland salmon mousse. However, for colour you cannot go past this roulade. If you don't overcook it, if you don't skimp on the saffron, and you don't use bland, cheap brie, then you will love it. The colour is a bright vibrant yellow, and the wonderfully peppery brie filling is superb — what could be nicer, and complement so many other flavours so well? An alternative filling is the wonderful homemade saffron ricotta opposite.

60 g (2 oz) butter, melted
⅓ cup flour
½ teaspoon saffron threads infused in ¾ cup milk
2 yellow peppers, roasted, skinned and puréed
3 eggs, separated
½ cup grated light cheese such as edam
salt and pepper

FILLING
250 g (8 oz) double-cream brie, softened
pinch of freshly ground white pepper

Method

Preheat the oven to 180°C/350°F. In a pan melt the butter, add the flour and cook the roux. Add the saffron-infused milk (including threads) and the pepper purée. Cook for 1 minute over gentle heat, being careful not to let the mixture catch on the base of the pot. Remove from the heat and beat in the egg yolks, cheese, salt and

Notes

As it is largely egg, the roulade will continue cooking when taken out of the oven, so experiment with your oven until you get the time right. An overcooked roulade loses its flavour, is dry, and can simply taste of burnt egg — not great, but very common.

Too much liquid in your roulade base will result in a roulade that will have difficulty holding. For example a tomato roulade rolled to enclose a white crab butter is best made from double sun-dried tomato paste, rather than fresh tomato, or roast your tomatoes in the oven, purée and sweat them down in a pan until a good dark paste is formed. Paprika may be needed to hold the colour.

The filling cannot be sloppy for cocktail food; something that will set when cooled is best. Cheese is excellent when added to fillings while they are warm. Other possibilities are breadcrumbs folded lightly through pesto, a small amount of unsalted butter melted and folded through seasoned crab or crayfish, pepper. Cool. Whip the egg whites until firm but not dry and fold them into the cooled egg-yolk mixture. Pour into a lined sponge-roll tin and bake for 10–12 minutes, until fluffy and golden brown.

Turn the roulade out onto a clean tea towel that has been dusted with freshly grated parmesan and a sprinkling of Maldon salt. Spread the softened brie onto the warm roulade, dust with the pepper and roll the roulade up from each end, so that you have two thin roulades. Cut down the middle and cool completely. Slice when firm, and serve.

Homemade *Saffron* Ricotta

Homemade ricotta is a beautiful cheese. This is a variation of a recipe created by Beverley Sutherland-Smith, who has a delightful school in Melbourne, where she has been teaching to full houses for almost 27 years. When I took 28 people on a tour across to the Food City of Australia, we headed straight for Beverley's school, where we enjoyed a fast, informative class that covered everything from a sweet potato gâteau to how to improve our cooking of seafood, from Japanese techniques in cooking chicken to blanching bean sprouts for a quick Korean salad.

This recipe is typical of Beverley's style — simple, no-fail and very up to date. I have altered the flavour slightly and increased the lemon juice just a little to complement the roulade. Try different flavours, add herbs and spices, or just make it plain and delicious.

Method

Soak the saffron threads in a little of the milk, then add this to the remainder. Put the saffron milk (including threads) and the cream in a saucepan and heat until it comes to the boil. Add the lemon juice a spoonful at a time and stir; the milk should form curds. Pull to the side of the stove and leave to stand for about 5 minutes. Line a colander with cheese cloth and place it over a large basin. Pour about half the mixture through, then the second half, so the curds settle gradually. Leave to stand for about 30 minutes; do not leave for too long or the cheese will become dry. This makes a great roulade filling.

½ teaspoon saffron threads
8 cups milk
1 cup cream
3–4 tablespoons lemon juice

---

a little aspic added to a base such as finely diced smoked chicken and herbs, or a hint of gelatine added to a smoked ham mousse that will be rolled in a roulade of roasted peach.

You need cocktail food with colour? Try some of these ideas. But always remember that it is only a smart cold omelette you are serving, so be generous either in your serving or at least in your seasoning.

Sorrel and lemon pepper roulade rolled to enclose scallops diced and lightly sautéed, then bound with a tiny amount of crème fraîche.

Roulade of black field mushrooms rolled to enclose a mixture of roasted red peppers puréed with malt vinegar, sautéed and enriched with a small amount of cream cheese.

Roulade of fresh thyme and orange with a duck liver or smoked pheasant pâté filling.

Smoked oyster and fine herb roulade rolled to enclose a white mushroom pâté. Serve with a truffled mayonnaise or apple aïoli (see Basics).

Grilled Radicchio *with* Chilli Beef

In my trips abroad I have managed several times to get to the classes of Mogens Bay Esbensen. Mogens has been involved in numerous restaurants, hotels and kitchens throughout the world, and although he is Danish by birth his food is anything but. He cooks classical, innovative and the most stunning Thai. A chef who cooks from the heart, he enjoys sharing recipes and ideas with keen cooks and, to top it all off, he has a wonderfully warped sense of humour. This finger food is inspired by the recipes he shared with me and by his great love of Thai flavours.

We love this recipe so much we make the sauce up in large amounts and store it in the larder for ease of use. It holds perfectly well out of the fridge but to have good colour add some fresh coriander and mint when you are ready to use it.

Combine the beef and the dressing at the last moment as the dressing is very high in salt and will quickly draw all the moisture out of the beef.

This recipe is excellent as a static finger-food dish. We pile a large brass tray with the tossed beef and surround it with small, crisp lettuce leaves so that guests can make their own little hors d'oeuvre rolls as they choose. We have used the sauce, thickened with a pinch of arrowroot, as an accompaniment to chicken mousse wontons. Using arrowroot as a thickening agent will give you an unctuous but clear sauce. Corn or wheat flour will cloud the sauce.

This is also a great sauce to make up and fold through any leftover beef, lamb, pork or chicken. Add a little to vegetables to sharpen up a steam-fry, use it to lift pumpkin and coconut soup, and have it as an accompaniment to chilli and roasted tomato salad.

2 cloves garlic, finely chopped
45 ml (1½ fl oz) soy sauce
45 ml (1½ fl oz) fresh lemon juice
20 ml (¾ fl oz) fish sauce (Nam Pla)
30 g (1 oz) brown sugar or palm sugar
¼ cup thinly sliced shallots
4 red chillies, seeded and cut into strips
4 tomatoes, skinned, seeded and chopped
500 g (1lb) lean cooked sirloin, rump or fillet steak, roasted to medium-rare
¼ cup finely chopped coriander
¼ cup mint leaves, rolled and sliced into thin strips
½ cup roughly chopped snowpea sprouts
2 radicchio lettuces, leaves separated and washed
12 chives, blanched and chilled

Method

Combine the garlic, soy sauce, lemon juice, Nam Pla and sugar. Mix well and fold in the shallots, chillies, and tomatoes. Slice the beef finely and toss in the marinade along with the coriander, mint and snowpea sprouts.

Place the radicchio leaves on a board, top with 1 tablespoon of the beef, and roll. Tie with the blanched chives, heat under a hot grill for 3 minutes, or until well coloured. Serve on platters with a little of the sauce drizzled to one side.

FABULOUS FINGER FOOD

Notes

When working with coriander remember to use the entire plant — the leaves, stems and roots all have great flavour. We would be inclined to add the finely chopped stems and roots to a sauce in the early stages, and at the last minute add the leaves so as to maintain colour and enrich the flavour. The ultimate in Thai cooking, no waste at all.

Radicchio grills beautifully on its own; just place the leaves, curved side up, on a baking tray, drizzle with olive oil, sprinkle with salt and place 10 cm (4 in) from the heat for about three minutes, or until soft. Spread with a small amount of well-flavoured blue cheese, some toasted walnuts and return to the oven until the cheese is just melted. A delicious appetiser, or accompaniment to a beef main course.

astonishing Appetisers & sensational Soups

Warm Mushroom Pâté with Apples and Cognac	46
Warm Marinated Salmon	47
Marbled Egg, Smoked Eel and Wasabi	48
Cauliflower and Orange Bisque	50
Bouillon of Autumn Mushrooms like a Cappucino	52
Canterbury Turnip and Blue Cheese Soup	54
Cream of Celery and Almond Soup	55
Peppered Scallop Bisque with Walnut Dumplings	56
Pumpkin, Brie and Scallop Bisque with Prosciutto	57
Soup Almondine	58
Onion and Oxtail Soup	59
Red Pepper and Pear Soup	61

Both the appetiser and the soup can be the beginning to a meal. Of course you may not have an appetiser, you may simply have a soup, but however you design your menu, these two courses should not be underrated.

Two years ago I organised and enjoyed the most perfect dinner at Michaels. Perhaps it was just perfect to me. I had chosen eight small courses, barely a tasting, of my favourite food from the current menu. It was a farewell dinner for a small weekend class we had held at the Small Kitchen School. There were ten at the dinner, the wines were chosen by Alan Overton, our resident wine buff and restaurant manager extraordinaire, and the combination of good friends, great conversation, and superb food and wine created an evening I shall never forget. From start to finish we took five hours, the shortest five hours of my life.

To begin such an evening it is important to have a small, well-flavoured course. Something to gently awaken the tastebuds and create a feeling of anticipation for the evening to come. Use perfectly cooked produce, light crisp flavours, and nothing heavy. Perhaps a pheasant salad served on a thin sliver of orange, or a small square of fresh trout with a dribble of citron oil and the slightest twist of lime. One fresh scallop barely cooked and served in its glistening shell with a slice of crisp apple, a turn of the pepper mill and a sprig of fennel. A quenelle of the most perfect watercress mousse you could imagine, served on a hint of red pepper coulis. Perhaps a flake of lightly cooked potato, a spoonful of the best caviar you can afford and a dusting of Maldon salt and white pepper.

Keep it small, fun and fresh. As your guests are only getting the faintest taste, make it perfect. Or don't make it at all. This course will be the first impression of the dinner and first impressions, as we all know, are very important. If you wish to have an entire dinner designed around appetisers, plan it carefully and try not to be too precious for the first experience. Don't panic if the hollandaise for that beautifully peeled spear of new season's asparagus has curdled past repair — just add a little orange zest and call it asparagus with rich scrambled eggs and orange. Keep strong red and

> '*Don't* panic if the hollandaise for that beautifully *peeled* spear of new season's *asparagus* has curdled past repair — just add a little *orange zest* and call it asparagus with *rich* scrambled *eggs* and orange.'

ASTONISHING APPETISERS & SENSATIONAL SOUPS

heavy gamey meat to a minimum, as it can overpower the entire evening. Have a good variety, but make sure that each course will marry in with the next. For example, a course of oven-roasted mushroom with essence of walnut could be followed perfectly with a breast of quail served on top of the most exquisite warm lentil salad.

Serve each course on oversized white plates, if you wish with a shot of something to accompany it — very cold but very good vodka, a small glass of dry chilled sherry, a flute of champagne or sparkling mineral water.

Increase the size of these recipes to create an entrée, reduce or simply adapt them to serve as an hors d'oeuvre, for in reality this course is only a cunning little canapé that has been plated.

Soup should always be designed for the occasion, the season and the menu as a whole. Cold soups are excellent in summer, especially when a hot entrée is to follow. I often make a chilled brandied apricot soup when relatives come for dinner; I am always very generous with the brandy, finish the soup with white wine, and manage to get everyone talking quite loudly before we even get to the next course. An excellent soup when entertaining guests you are worried about — or when you want them to feel so good about the meal that they won't bring up your oh-so-joyful adolescence yet again.

Soup is a very welcoming dish. A good hearty soup in winter always makes me feel as if someone has given me a big, warm, fuzzy cuddle. An elegant, thin soup, on the other hand, makes you sit up in anticipation of a dinner to come. Some soups suit large oatmeal bowls, some delicate silver one-handled coupes, and others pottery mugs. Choose whatever suits your occasion or your personality, whichever is the more important to you.

Warm Mushroom Pâté *with* Apple *and* Cognac

In my early days of owning Michaels Restaurant I was very lucky to have a chef who was the most brilliant target for practical jokes. Ngaire could cook, she could get meals out and do the dishes all at the same time, and boy did it help keep staff costs down. Between the two of us we would have the kitchen looking spotless, the benches polished and the meals quietly rolling out to the customers, and all along we would be busy thinking what dirty trick we could play on each other at the end of the day. I haven't had so much fun in a kitchen since. Walkie-talkies hidden behind the staff toilet cistern, surprise wind-up spiders tucked under tea towels, fire extinguishers booby-trapped to spray as you walked past, and ice discreetly tucked down your trousers while you were talking to a client on the phone. Surprise wake-up calls at six in the morning, and worst of all, a surprise breakfast party in my house at seven in the morning with all the staff, their partners and all — and me unable to get out of bed as the result of there being too many people around and my having too little clothing on. In fact, when I think about it I am sure I still owe Ngaire one more dirty prank.

This recipe we created together when after a great staff picnic we had collected a lot of mushrooms — or rather had acquired mushrooms from some unsuspecting farmer's paddock. They were dark, small, and smelt just wonderful. Young enough not to have those horrible little lice, but we soaked them in salt water and put them through the lettuce spinner before cooking just to make sure.

When making this recipe be very generous with your seasonings. As the pâté is served warm both the mushroom and the apple absorb a lot of flavour, and they need that extra kick from the nutmeg and the bacon. If you are making it in advance taste it before warming it to serve. White pepper is often required, and a generous pinch of Maldon or sea salt may also be necessary.

Method

Dice the bacon and fry it until crisp. Drain and set to one side. Add half the butter to the fat rendered by the bacon, and to this add the diced mushrooms, shallots and apple. Cook for about 12 minutes. Season with nutmeg, pepper and lightly with salt. Blend all to a purée, melt and add the remaining butter, and add the Cognac. Check the seasoning.

Serve the pâté piled into a large ramekin and accompanied by savoury tuiles, madeleines, fresh hot toast fingers or perhaps fingers of grilled sourdough bread.

Notes

This pâté holds well and can be made in advance, reheated, reseasoned and quenelled just prior to eating. Field mushrooms will give you a delicious black pâté, while farmed buttons will give you a creamy-white pâté. Both are excellent.

We stuff steaks with this pâté, use it layered in a gratin of autumn vegetables, at cocktail parties as a filling for wontons, as a little tartlet filling and puréed as a dip for marinated chicken kebabs. We fill herbed brioche with it for a supper menu and add it to terrines when we have any left over.

Another mushroom appetiser we have used when catering is small field mushrooms filled with a well flavoured pumpkin and parmesan conserve, heated and served in a similar style to the recipe above but with crisp oven-dried paper-thin pumpkin flakes. The flavour is intense, the colour is very dramatic, and the dish can be served hot, warm or cold. A caterer's dream dish when the ovens decide to die in the middle of service.

250 g (8 oz) streaky bacon
125 g (4 oz) butter
500 g (1 lb) mushrooms, diced
60 g (2 oz) shallots, chopped
2 eating apples, peeled, cored and coarsely chopped
1 generous pinch nutmeg
freshly ground white pepper to taste
Maldon or sea salt to taste
2 soup spoons Cognac

ASTONISHING APPETISERS & SENSATIONAL SOUPS

Warm Marinated Salmon

One of the most popular appetisers is fresh salmon. Catch your own if you can; it's a very relaxing sport. Just take along some good music, a hip flask of gin and tonic, and absolutely no portable phone. But if time or patience are not on your side, New Zealand farm salmon is excellent, fresh and well flavoured. It can be supplied without any pin bones, a great blessing for the shortsighted.

This is an appetiser we use a lot because of its simplicity, its flavour and its texture.

Method

Chill the salmon to firm up the flesh and make it easier to work with. With the skin side down and using a sharp knife, slice the salmon into thin slices, cutting on the slant towards the tail. Cut enough to cover 4 dinner plates, flatten if necessary with a clean plate, cover with plastic wrap and refrigerate until just before serving.

Combine all the other ingredients and drizzle over the fish 5 minutes before serving.

Place in a 180°C/350°F oven for 2 minutes and serve warm, topped with a little rock salt. Serve with mayonnaise to which you have added a splash of cream, and sprinkle over some freshly chopped chives or spring onions.

250 g (8 oz) boneless salmon
125 ml (4 fl oz) peanut oil
½ teaspoon fresh ginger, peeled and finely chopped
1 teaspoon pink peppercorns
½ teaspoon salt
juice and zest of 1 lemon

Notes

A good way to serve this salmon is in the middle of either a large white plate or on a well-polished silver charger, with a thin slice of lemon, half dipped in black pepper and the other half in finely chopped herbs. A light dusting of paprika on the plate is the only addition needed.

I have also served this as the accompaniment to a creamy fresh salmon bisque, piled in the middle of the plate with the soup poured gently around. Accompanied with herbed brioche, the three elements blend very well.

This is an easy recipe for just about any fish. Monkfish would be one of my favourites, and when presented in this manner it is mild and succulent.

Marbled Egg, Smoked Eel *and* Wasabi

As with finger food, you can be a little more creative with appetisers than with main courses as guests tend to be more venturesome with one mouthful than with a whole plateful of something new. It is the time to be original, exotic and innovative. This dish just goes to show what can be made from the most simple ingredients. Free-range eggs from the neighbour's chickens, some fresh eel caught the night before and smoked over manuka, and wasabi, believe it or not, grown locally in Canterbury.

It is a delightful appetiser, with the eggs looking very much like the Italian marble eggs that are sold as paperweights, the superb flavour of creamy smoked-eel mousse, and the sharpness of wasabi. A combination that works beautifully not only on the tastebuds but on the eye as well, this is a dish that lends itself to both classical and modern interpretations.

Smoked eel has a delicate, almost earthy, flavour which does need the seasoning of the wasabi to give it some body.

ASTONISHING APPETISERS & SENSATIONAL SOUPS

If you cannot get smoked eel try a local hot smoked white fish or even some hot smoked salmon. Do remember to alter your seasoning to suit the fish.

Be gentle with wasabi. I love it, and enjoy that burst of flavour as your mouth explodes and your eyes start to run. However, your guests may like to have some tastebuds left so they can enjoy the rest of the evening. It is wise to caution them to go gently at first, tasting just a little with their smoked-eel mousse. Wasabi can be bought commercially in paste or powder form which, although not as strong as fresh wasabi, still has a good flavour. Horseradish is a poor substitute, but perfectly acceptable.

Marbled Eggs

6 eggs
1 tablespoon sea salt
2 teaspoons saffron threads
1 teaspoon turmeric

Boil the eggs for 15 minutes and leave them to cool in their shells. Once cold, tap the eggs all over with the back of a spoon, until they are completely crazed. Sit the eggs gently in a small pot, add the salt, saffron and turmeric, and cover with cold water. Bring to the boil, reduce the heat and simmer slowly for 2–3 hours, adding more water as needed. Turn the heat off and leave the eggs to cool in the liquid for at least 6 hours; do not take them out of their shells until you are ready to use them. These will keep well wrapped in the fridge for about 5 days.

Smoked Eel Mousse

200 g (7 oz) smoked eel, finely chopped
1/4 cup sour cream
60 g (2 oz) cream cheese
1/4 teaspoon white pepper
2 teaspoons freshly squeezed lemon juice
1/8 teaspoon wasabi or prepared wasabi paste (to accompany)
1/4 teaspoon horseradish paste

Combine all the ingredients thoroughly in a stainless steel or ceramic bowl and leave for about an hour for the flavours to mingle. Check seasoning and sharpen if necessary with lemon juice.

TO SERVE
Carefully peel the eggs, take the top off gently and scoop out all the yolk and a thin layer of the firm white. Sit the egg in a silver eggcup. With 2 warm teaspoons quenelle the smoked-eel mousse and place it inside the egg, with the top just showing. Place the eggcup in the middle of a large white plate and a teaspoon of wasabi paste to one side. If you like, the egg yolk can be finely chopped and placed in a pile on the plate with the wasabi. A fresh sprig of chervil would look perfect.

Notes

Fresh horseradish is one of the horrors of cooking. My sister Cherry grows it for me and brings it into the kitchens in large wooden trays. Those in the know are suddenly very busy and we all wait for some poor unsuspecting staff member to offer to wash, grate and prepare it for storage. To do a good job you must scrape the radish, grate it, then store it in a little vinegar. You develop a rash from head to toe, your eyes run, and your hands, face and anywhere else you touch burns. People who have done it once by hand grate it carefully through the kitchen whizz with all the doors open around them. They are careful not to handle it too much, if at all, and I am sure they can all now hold their breath for five minutes before running outside for fresh air. They use plastic bags on their hands, and one of my pantry staff has been known to wear a gauze face mask. Like garlic, chillies and Asian fermented shrimp paste, it is all vital to the finished product. Sometimes you just have to put up with the hassle to get the goods.

Cauliflower *and* Orange Bisque

60 g (2 oz) butter
250 g (8 oz) cauliflower florets
125 g (4 oz) onion, finely chopped
125 g (4 oz) leeks, finely chopped
125 g (4 oz) celery, finely chopped
60 g (2 oz) potatoes, finely chopped
125 g (4 oz) whole blanched almonds, coarsely chopped
60 g (2 oz) plain flour
1 bouquet garni (bayleaf, thyme, peppercorns)
600 ml (1 pint) light chicken stock
300 ml (½ pint) orange juice
450 ml (¾ pint) milk
150 ml (¼ pint) cream
salt and freshly ground black pepper
2 tablespoons yoghurt
1 tablespoon chopped parsley
4 oranges, segmented

One of the highlights of being a cook and travelling is meeting people who are absolutely passionate about food. Author, food writer and teacher Joanne Weir is one of the most passionate and amazing foodies I have met. She looks after me when I am in San Francisco, she is young, beautiful, and man, can she cook Mediterranean food 'to die for'. Her methods and techniques come from her great love of food, her training with such people as Madeleine Kamman at Berringer in Napa Valley and with Alice Waters at Chez Panisse. When Joanne cooks you want to cry, then when you think about it, she is just so good you want to kill her. Her flavours are honest, crisp and exciting, and she is one of the most approachable talents I have had the pleasure of meeting.

This soup has absolutely nothing to do with Joanne. It is a soup I put together after a trip to San Francisco. I decided that yoghurt would be great with cauliflower, and the addition of orange would sharpen up what is often a mild and unexciting soup. It is great in that you do not have to blend it, it will hold well, although the cauliflower will soften, but the flavour will improve. Add extra cauliflower florets when you reheat it to keep the crunch, or purée the soup and fold in some fresh orange and finely chopped herbs to create a different kind of look.

Method

Melt the butter in a large, heavy-based pan. Add the cauliflower, onion, leeks, celery, potatoes and coarsely chopped almonds, cover, and sweat until transparent but not coloured. Stir in the flour and cook gently for 5 minutes.

Add the bouquet garni, stock, orange juice and milk. Cover and simmer for about 30 minutes. Remove the bouquet garni. Stir in the cream and season with salt and pepper to taste.

Divide between warmed soup plates and swirl in the yoghurt. Sprinkle with chopped parsley, garnish with orange and serve immediately.

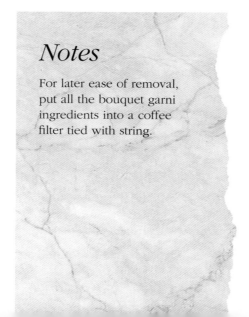

Notes

For later ease of removal, put all the bouquet garni ingredients into a coffee filter tied with string.

ASTONISHING APPETISERS & SENSATIONAL SOUPS

Bouillon *of* Autumn Mushrooms *like a* Cappuccino

This soup was used at a winter dinner for the Gourmet Society at Michaels. It is an excellent way to serve a large number of people and a very easy soup to put together. The froth at serving time is a little bit of a hassle but well worth the effort.

It is a rich soup that can be enriched further with walnuts, lightened with stock or finished with extra cream. I personally like this with the champagne bread. Not only is the bread very easy to make, and its sweetness goes well with mushrooms, it is great toasted in the morning for breakfast. Instead of using mushrooms, a cappuccino of parsnip with a froth of bacon-enriched milk is exquisite — just right for a winter dinner.

60 g (2 oz) butter
30 g (1 oz) finely chopped walnuts
250 g (8 oz) button mushrooms, wiped
1.2 l (2 pints) light chicken stock
300 ml (½ pint) cream
salt and cayenne to flavour
200 g (6 oz) seafood (crayfish, scallops, prawns etc.)
fish stock to poach
30 g (1 oz) butter
125 g (4 oz) dried mushrooms (shiitake, oyster or morel mushrooms), soaked
3 tablespoons brandy
1 teaspoon finely chopped fresh tarragon

Method

Heat the 60 g (2 oz) butter in a large saucepan, add the walnuts and cook until they have coloured lightly. Chop the button mushrooms finely and add them to the butter and walnuts, cooking gently for 5 minutes. Add the stock and cream, and leave to simmer on a low heat for another 10 minutes to infuse the flavours and reduce the liquid by a quarter. Add the salt and cayenne to flavour. Strain, keeping the liquid hot and the finely chopped mushroom/walnuts to one side.

In a separate pan poach the shellfish in the fish stock for 1–2 minutes, until it is just opaque. Drain, shell the fish and coarsely chop it.

In a small frypan heat the 30 g (1 oz) butter, add the dried mushrooms that have been rinsed and finely chopped. Add the shellfish and brandy and flambé, then add the tarragon and mushroom/walnut mixture. Divide this mixture among six cappuccino cups and keep warm.

Froth the boiling stock and cream mixture in a blender. This gives the creamy soup a cappuccino-like head. Pour into the cups and serve with crayfish-buttered toast fingers.

Champagne Bread

Preheat the oven to 180°C/350°F. In a large bowl, combine the flour, sugar and sparkling wine. Cover with plastic wrap and leave to stand in a warm place until it begins to rise, about 30 minutes. Place the dough in a buttered loaf pan and let it continue to rise for another 30 minutes. Drizzle melted butter over the top of the loaf. Bake for 50-60 minutes, or until golden brown.

3 cups self-raising flour
⅓ cup sugar
1½ cups sparkling wine
60 g (2 oz) butter, melted

Notes

This recipe works best with chilled sparkling wine that has just been opened. If the wine is at all flat, add 3 teaspoons of baking powder to the recipe.

ASTONISHING APPETISERS & SENSATIONAL SOUPS

Notes

To make crayfish butter, crush the shells of crayfish with a small amount of butter and water, put this over a low heat and let it simmer for about five minutes. Drain the butter and water mixture and let cool, throwing out the sieved crayfish shells. Once the butter has set remove the water and discard. The butter will be a pale orange colour, with a good crayfish flavour. Add a squeeze of lemon, a pinch of salt and cayenne and the butter is just perfect for croûtons, as an addition to fish sauces or to enrich a seafood soup.

Canterbury Turnip *and* Blue Cheese Soup

I had never been a fan of turnip soup. The flavour didn't appeal to me greatly, and too often I would remember that it was basically cattle fodder, dug up from the house paddock and thrown together in a desperate attempt to feed the hungry. Another one of those low-budget wonders.

So when I was served this soup by Lyn, a delightfully off-beat aunt who lives in Auckland, I was most impressed. She wisely omitted to tell me that it was based on turnip until after my first taste, and I must admit that after that initial spoonful I was hooked. No doubt the turnips were from the dairy farm up at Wellsford and the blue cheese from Kapiti. The recipe was so simple, with very few ingredients, and the amount of blue cheese in the soup very small, although this is lifted by the addition of the blue cheese croûtons. My aunt also had the brilliant idea of adding good-sized splashes of brandy at regular intervals as we ate. I must admit it was addictive, and since then I have frequently been seen sitting at a small table in the dark at Michaels, quietly getting through the odd bowl or two.

Method

Melt the butter and add the turnip, onion and potato. Allow the vegetables to sweat for 10 minutes, then add the stock and 2 tablespoons of blue cheese. Simmer for about 15 minutes, until the vegetables are soft. Allow to cool, purée then reheat. Add the nutmeg and salt and pepper to taste. Thin the mixture with cream, if preferred.

Mix the 60 g (2 oz) blue cheese and 30 g (1 oz) butter together and spread over the French bread. Bake in a moderate oven until lightly coloured. Sprinkle with cracked black pepper and place one slice in the base of each soup bowl. Pour the hot soup over and serve garnished with fresh parsley.

60 g (2 oz) butter
900 g (1½ lb) finely sliced white turnip
1 large onion, finely sliced
1 large potato, finely sliced
900 ml (1½ pints) chicken stock
2 tablespoons blue cheese
¼ teaspoon freshly ground nutmeg
salt and pepper to taste
1½ cups cream (optional)
60 g (2 oz) blue cheese
30 g (1 oz) butter
6 slices French bread
parsley for garnish

Notes

This soup relies on good stock, so if you are making your own or enriching a bought stock with additional flavour, do make it good and strong. See the Basics section for notes on stocks.

ASTONISHING APPETISERS & SENSATIONAL SOUPS

Cream *of* Celery *and* Almond Soup

If being hard up has taught me nothing else, it has taught me that some of the very best dishes can be made with the cheapest ingredients. This is in a sense a return to my mother's cooking style, where if produce wasn't in the garden or on special at the local shop then it sure as eggs did not appear at the table. My mother had such a tight grip on the money that if she ran out of flour to thicken a dish she used potato, ran out of vanilla to enrich a very light custard (a two-egg custard to feed eight) she used geranium leaves; she always used honey instead of sugar, top milk instead of cream and, well before her time, and solely to save money, she cut back on salt, butter and eggs in all her cooking. But what my mother could do with a kilo of potatoes, the vegetable trimmings and a pile of old bacon bones was unbelievable.

This recipe was originally made using the base of the celery; potatoes were used to thicken it, and milk to finish it. I have added the extra almonds, finished it with cream, and incorporated butter — after all, I'm going on a diet tomorrow and this could just be one of my last good meals.

This soup is perfect for any season as it can be served hot, warm and, if well flavoured, even chilled. Decorate the top with toasted almonds, add a spoonful of crème fraîche or sour cream, or simply dust with herbs.

1 teaspoon olive oil
60 g (2 oz) flaked almonds
2 tablespoons butter
1 large onion, diced
4 cups finely chopped celery
4 tablespoons whole blanched almonds
5 cups light chicken stock
60 g (2 oz) butter
60 g (2 oz) flour
½–1 cup spinach purée (optional)
½ pint milk
1 pint cream
salt and pepper

Method

In a sauté pan heat the olive oil and when hot add the flaked almonds. Cook over a gentle heat until the almonds are a light golden colour, taking care not to overcook them or they will be bitter. Tip out and cool, putting them to one side for garnish.

In a large pot sweat the onion, celery and almonds with 2 tablespoons butter for about 3 minutes. Add the stock and simmer until all are tender. Cool slightly and purée.

In a large saucepan heat the 60 g (2 oz) butter. When it has melted and stopped sizzling add the flour and cook for 2 minutes, or until it smells cooked but has not coloured. To this roux add the puréed soup mixture and blend in the spinach, milk and cream to taste. Bring to a simmer, season well and serve with the flaked almonds as garnish.

Notes

This soup freezes well but may split when thawed. To repair this, add a little cornflour slackened with milk as you reheat and the soup will come together. Do re-season.

If the celery mixture has too light a colour for your liking, add some spinach purée. At both the restaurant and catering company we purée fresh spinach and freeze it in ice cubes, keeping them in large bags and taking out as many as we need to repair or enrich a sauce. We do the same with basil, fresh mint when there is a flush, and lime juice and zest as they seem very seasonal.

Peppered Scallop Bisque *with* Walnut Dumplings

I created this dish when involved in a formal dinner for some little titled bunny coming out from England. Scallops they wanted, Nelson ones of course, the soup needed to be well flavoured, and as it was likely to be a cool day they wanted just a little substance in the soup. Well, with 20 kilos of scallops given to us to practise with, I was obviously keen. It might need Cognac I said, and sure as eggs, two bottles of good Cognac arrived. This is magic, could we use truffles, I thought, but that was taking it a little far — as it was I had no intention of putting the Cognac in the soup.

This is the basic soup, which I was quite happy with, but for the formal occasion we sliced and very lightly seared some extra scallops, tossed them with a few drops of tabasco and piled them into the middle of the soup plate, sat three little walnut dumplings around, some fresh herbs, and poured the soup over and around. It looked like a castle with a moat of soup. Quite grand I thought, and it tasted just heavenly to boot.

1.8 l (3 pints) fish stock
90 g (3 oz) butter
125 g (4 oz) mirepoix (see Notes)
¼ teaspoon lightly crushed white peppercorns
90 g (3 oz) flour
½ cup dry vermouth
250 g (8 oz) scallops, roe separated
300 ml (½ pint) cream

Method

Place the fish stock in a pot and bring to a simmer.

In another pot melt the butter and sweat the vegetables until they are soft but not coloured. Add the peppercorns and flour and cook for 2 minutes. Add the vermouth and hot stock and simmer for about 5 minutes. Finely dice the roe of the scallops and fold into the soup. Add the diced scallops and cream and season to taste. Do not boil.

Tomato paste, fresh fennel, lemon juice and white wine can be used to heighten the flavours if necessary. This soup depends a lot on having a good fish stock.

Walnut *Dumplings*

1 cup flour
2 teaspoons baking powder
½ teaspoon salt
½ cup milk
2 tablespoons walnut oil
1 tablespoon finely zested lemon
2 tablespoons toasted walnuts, finely chopped
1 tablespoon finely chopped parsley
1 tablespoon finely chopped chives, fennel or tarragon

Combine the flour, baking powder and salt in a bowl. Mix the milk, oil, lemon, walnuts and herbs together and add them to the bowl. Stir the mixture just enough to moisten the dry ingredients evenly.

Drop teaspoonfuls of batter into the simmering soup, about 1 cm (½ in) apart. Cover the pan tightly and cook, undisturbed, for 8–10 minutes — until the dumplings are firm and cooked in the centre and have risen to the top of the liquid.

Notes

To me a mirepoix is a mixture of two parts each of diced carrot and onion to one part celery, and sometimes a small amount of leek, cooked in butter in a saucepan. This combination is all I find necessary in my sauces, although other chefs sometimes include bacon, pork fat and even parsley and garlic, as in an Italian-influenced mirepoix, sometimes called 'battuto'.

Dumplings can be made much lighter by using choux pastry and adding egg white. (See the notes on Chicken Almondine, page 29.)

If you are making up the soup and do not intend to eat it straight away, do not add the scallops until the soup has been reheated. In this way you do not overcook the scallops and get those flavourless little nuggets that are so often served in a soup that has been held hot to within an inch of its life.

Pumpkin, Brie *and* Scallop Bisque with Prosciutto

This pumpkin, scallop and prosciutto soup with brie is another unusual combination, but all the flavours marry together very well — the richness of the pumpkin and brie, the subtlety of the barely cooked scallops and the crispness of the grilled prosciutto. This soup is popular with skiers; we place it in thermos flasks in the hampers, along with freshly baked parsley bread, often a small terrine of marinated roast chicken, crisp noodle and roasted tomato salad, and a thick slice of chocolate mousse gâteau. Skiing is such a popular pastime in Canterbury that we have now employed extra winter staff just to organise, cook and deliver these hampers to eager clients. I am certain this soup is the main reason for their success.

Method

Sauté the onion in the butter until lightly coloured. Add the chicken stock and cook for about 2 minutes. Whisk in the pumpkin purée and brie, and fold in the diced pumpkin. Add the scallops, cream and seasoning. Bring to a tremble and hold. While you are doing this frizzle the prosciutto and hold to one side. When sautéed, prosciutto only becomes crisp as it cools, so fry it until some of the fat has been released and the prosciutto has darkened, place on a kitchen towel and drain. Crumble for garnish.

Pour the soup into warm soup bowls. The large flat oatmeal/pasta style are great. Pile the frizzled prosciutto on top and serve with perhaps a bowl of crisp croûtons, well-dried French bread or old-fashioned white sliced bread toasted and piled into a linen napkin on the table.

Notes

If this soup is to be made ahead and reheated for dinner in the evening, add the scallops and well-chilled diced brie just prior to reheating. This will ensure you do not overcook the scallops and dissolve the brie. Leaving the rind of the brie on will give you a stronger flavour, but the look may not be so good. I often freeze the brie and grate it, keeping it frozen and adding it to the soup in the last stage. This gives a good texture and guarantees that the soup will still have some texture and flavour from the brie as you enjoy the meal.

90 g (3 oz) butter
2 large onions, finely chopped
4–6 cups light chicken stock
1 cup roasted, skinned and puréed pumpkin
2 small rounds diced brie (well chilled)
1 cup steamed and diced pumpkin
250 g (8 oz) scallops, coarsely chopped
cream to finish (optional)
rock salt and cracked white pepper to taste
90 g (3 oz) prosciutto (for garnish)

Soup Almondine

This soup was created for a client's dinner party; it had to look good on the new dinner service, show up the 'had to be noticed' cutlery, and be subtle and tasteful just like the cook — or did she say host — to this day I am not sure. It is such a simple soup to make, using only one pot, a hand-held blender and an element — a kitchenhand's dream when it comes to cleaning up. Again, a soup that relies on good stock, preferably well flavoured but light in colour.

Method

Melt the butter in a large saucepan over a gentle heat. Cook the onions and coarsely chopped almonds together, making sure they do not colour. Add the chicken stock, potatoes, salt and white pepper. Simmer until the potatoes are tender then, with a hand-held blender (see Notes) or a vitamiser, blend until smooth. If serving straight away add all the remaining ingredients and pour into warmed soup bowls. If you are reheating the soup, these last ingredients are best added once the blended soup has regained its heat. Do check the seasoning, as reheating can alter the flavour a little. Parsley is an excellent garnish.

This soup can be frozen at the first stage, but may look curdled when defrosted. Gently heat it to boiling point, and beat with a whisk, and the soup will regain its texture. A little slackened cornflour may be needed to draw the soup together and a dash of butter whisked in at the eleventh hour will give it a good gloss.

60 g (2 oz) butter
2 large onions, coarsely chopped
1 cup almonds, coarsely chopped
5 cups strong chicken stock
2–3 large potatoes, coarsely chopped
salt and white pepper
4 teaspoons grated orange zest
300 ml (½ pint) cream
1 cup cooked chicken, diced
1 avocado, diced (optional)
1 tablespoon grated orange zest
4 tablespoons toasted slivered almonds
parsley

Notes

The hand-held beater we refer to affectionately as Wanda, or more professionally, the wand. It is a very useful tool that should be part of any cook's collection of kitchen equipment. The blender resembles an electric hand mixer, with a long thin wand and a rotary blade at the end; it is excellent for whipping, blending, puréeing and liquefying. I use mine regularly for soups such as this, plunging the blender directly into the pot, which means there is no need to transfer the liquids to a bowl or blender then back to the pot. It is a neat, almost magical, tool, superb for getting sauces creamy, disguising the fact that the roux may have gone a little lumpy, or for thickening a sauce with beurre manié (kneaded butter). For a perfect sauce, however, I would still pass it through a sieve to get that little extra air and lightness.

Onion *and* Oxtail Soup

Onion and oxtail is one of my favourite winter soups. It is a true country combination, and substantial enough to be served with damper scones for a hearty winter lunch or Sunday tea. We designed this soup for a client's fortieth birthday party. It was held in the heart of a very cold winter in a grand old home at the end of a two-and-a-half-hour drive. We started the dinner with this dish to warm everyone up. The host was a beef breeder, had one of the largest collections of red wines I had seen and was an enthusiastic cook, so this recipe seemed perfect. We served the soup in large old family oatmeal plates, garnished with thinly sliced caramelised onions and with large napkin-lined baskets of freshly baked breads and herb butters. It was a great success and we have used the soup regularly in winter ever since.

Method

The day before, begin by preparing the beef stock. Put the oxtails in a stockpot with enough water to cover. Bring to a simmer and add the carrots, celery, garlic, herbs, salt, and peppercorns. Simmer for 2–3 hours, covered. Strain the broth into a saucepan, and season with additional salt to taste. Remove the meat from the oxtails and dice it into 5 mm ($\frac{1}{4}$ in) pieces to make 1 cup. Refrigerate overnight.

The next day, remove the fat and bring the stock to a simmer. Melt the butter in a large saucepan. Add the onions and cook over medium-low heat, stirring often, for 25 minutes, until they become soft and golden brown. Sprinkle in the flour and cook for another couple of minutes. Remove from the heat and add the hot beef broth, whisking to combine the flour. Return to the heat, add the port and reserved diced meat, cover, and simmer for 15 minutes.

Preheat the grill. Combine all the cheeses in a bowl. Toast the slices of bread on both sides under the grill. Divide them among 4 flameproof soup bowls and fill each bowl with soup. Arrange the cheese over the top and slide the bowls under the grill, close to the heat source, grilling just long enough to lightly brown the cheese. Serve immediately.

1.5 kg (3 lb) beef oxtails, cut into small pieces
water to cover
4 carrots, peeled and halved
4 stalks celery, cut into large pieces
4 cloves garlic, peeled
4 sprigs fresh thyme
4 sprigs Italian (flat-leaf) parsley
1 teaspoon salt plus additional to taste
6 black peppercorns
90 g (3 oz) butter
500 g (1 lb) onions, peeled and thinly sliced
1 tablespoon flour
½ cup port
90 g (3 oz) gruyère, grated
60 g (2 oz) mozzarella, grated
2 tablespoons grated parmesan
4 x 2 cm (1 in) thick slices French bread

Butter and cream in soups

We've all become so afraid of using butter and cream that we seem to forget the simplest trick of all. Adding a touch of cream and butter just before serving makes for a soup that tastes rich without being indulgent.

Notes

Red peppers can be roasted either under a very hot grill or directly over a gas flame. To roast, rotate the peppers with tongs until they are completely blackened. Place them in a paper bag or wrap them in paper towels to 'sweat' for 5–10 minutes. Rub off the charred skin and remove the seeds.

Red Pepper *and* Pear Soup

Red pepper and pear soup is magical. We often serve this with a crisp fried julienne of ginger, a small bowl of crème fraîche, and oven-roasted thinly sliced pear. It is a most unusual combination, but typical of my recipes — it is not set in concrete, and should not be followed slavishly. For example, you may not share my love of parsnips, pears and garlic — so, simply cut down on the amount, or even substitute something else. Try the recipe as is first, then chop and change to get exactly the flavour you want. Who knows, you may create your own inspired original, and instead of giving me the credit you can keep all the praise for yourself. Cooking is never static and no one owns the recipe. Take courage, a good glass of wine and cook!

Parsnips are one of the most underrated vegetables. Combining them with red peppers and moist, juicy pears is something to blow your tiny boiler.

Method

Seed, core, and thinly slice 3 red peppers and set them aside. Roast the other 3 (see Note) and slice thinly.

Melt the butter in a large, heavy saucepan. Sauté the unroasted red peppers, shallots, garlic and pears over low heat for about 10 minutes, until tender but not browned. Add the parsnips and chicken stock, bring to a boil, and simmer until the parsnips are very tender, about 35–40 minutes. Allow to cool slightly.

Purée the mixture with a hand-held blender or in a food processor. Blend until smooth, adding 2 of the roasted peppers. Season with salt and pepper. Return to the saucepan and reheat.

To serve, place several small dollops of crème fraîche (see Basics) on top of the soup and, using a kitchen knife, swirl it through. Garnish with a strip of the reserved roasted pepper and a coriander leaf. This soup may also be served at room temperature.

6 sweet red peppers
6 tablespoons butter
6 shallots or little onions, peeled and minced
4 garlic cloves, peeled and minced
3 ripe pears, peeled, seeded, and cut into chunks
1 kg (2 lb) parsnips, peeled and cut into chunks
2 l (3¼ pints) chicken stock, preferably homemade
salt and freshly ground black pepper to taste
approximately ½ cup crème fraîche, to garnish
fresh coriander leaves, to garnish

extraordinary

Pistachio Chicken with Orange Mustard Sauce	65
Herbed Rabbit Clafoutis with Fresh Grape Chutney	66
Terrine of New Potato, Thyme and Double-Cream Brie with a Water Vinaigrette	68
Red Wine Confit with Green Garlic Souffle	70
Toasted Ravioli with Tomato Rosemary Sauce	72
Avocado and Sugar-Cured Bacon Wrapped in Yoghurt Pastry	74
Galette of Leek with Fig Tapenade and Salad of Lamb Shoulder	76
Coriander Tuiles with Pickled Grilled Scallops	78

Entrées

MICHAEL LEE-RICHARDS ❧ COOK!

A formal dinner may have four or five courses, a less formal occasion perhaps only two. A luncheon would be light, and consist of a small first course with fruit and cheese to finish, and a brunch may consist of a one-plate meal with coffee. Whatever the occasion, the meal needs a defined beginning, middle and end, and it is the small courses of finger food, appetisers and entrées that give you wonderful scope for being really imaginative.

From these small courses you can create numerous combinations for entertaining — combinations that suit you and your guests, and combinations that will fascinate, surprise and hopefully introduce something new. Planning a menu can be fun, and like many cooks I like to think of it as an art in which taste, shape, colour, texture and aroma interact to create a dramatic whole.

Traditionally courses for a dinner grow bigger as the meal progresses and move from light flavours to stronger. Although the appetiser is seen as a palate teaser, the entrée, being slightly larger, is considered the springboard to the main course. It should be teasing to the tastebuds, look great, and provide a contrast to what is to follow. It should not be too strong in flavour or overspiced.

If you have already served a rich creamy soup, you may consider a seafood salad with citrus sorbet or perhaps a dandelion salad with grapefruit; if the soup was light, an appropriate entrée might be mushrooms baked in crisp puff pastry, or the thinnest slice of the terrine of double-cream brie with fresh thyme.

Whichever way you design your menu, the aim surely is to present a delicious meal with a certain ease. Remember, a dinner, formal or informal, inside or outside, early supper or late meal, is a pause at the end of a long day. It should above all provide a few hours of ease for you and your guests.

Entrées, often simply called first courses, can be excellent as luncheon dishes or as a late supper, without too much alteration. They are perfect as a light meal on their own, and two entrées instead of an entrée and main course, or an entrée and dessert, totally avoiding the heavier main course, is becoming quite common.

In my travels abroad I often do a restaurant hop, having entrées in perhaps three restaurants and dessert and coffee in the fourth. This is a great way to look at menu styles, interiors and service without having to eat your way through several main courses. ❧

EXTRAORDINARY ENTRÉES

Pistachio Chicken *with* Orange Mustard Sauce

Is there anything better than crisp golden chips of moist chicken, dusted with pistachio and served with sharp mustard sauce? This is one of the quickest methods of cooking chicken; it is wonderfully fast, and if the oil is hot and you are careful not to overcook it, you'll have moist, juicy chicken. Remember that the chicken will continue to cook after it has been removed from the oil so less is best, timing wise. Finish it for a few minutes in the oven if you are worried.

I first tasted this sauce with almond-crusted king prawns. The flavour was exquisite. Like chicken, the prawns must be carefully cooked, the coating should be a lovely golden colour, and the sauce should be at room temperature. I much prefer this with chicken but do try other meats, vegetables and seafoods — the scope is limitless. The sauce is very simple to make and holds for several weeks in the refrigerator.

Orange Mustard Sauce

500 g (1 lb) sweet orange marmalade
¼ cup chicken stock
1 tablespoon lemon juice
½ teaspoon dry mustard
½ teaspoon chilli sauce
150 ml (¼ pint) fresh orange juice
1 tablespoon Dijon mustard
1 tablespoon blanched orange zest

Place all the ingredients in a pot and heat gently. Bring to the boil and cook until thickened slightly. Store in an airtight container in the fridge.

Pistachio *Chicken*

6 breasts of chicken, skin removed and cut into batons (chips)
1 cup flour
fine zest of 2 oranges
finely ground sea salt and white pepper
1 cup peeled chopped pistachios
½ cup toasted white breadcrumbs
3 eggs
3 tablespoons orange juice
60 g (2 oz) melted butter
2 cups safflower or grapeseed oil

Combine the flour, zest of 2 oranges, salt and pepper, and put onto a tray. Combine the pistachios and the toasted breadcrumbs in another tray, and the eggs with the orange juice and melted butter in another.

Flour, egg and crumb the chips of chicken and chill well. Heat the oil to 180°C/350°F and quickly cook the chicken in small batches for about 1 minute, placing it on paper towels and keeping it warm in a low oven until ready to serve. These chips are best served immediately as the chicken loses its delicious glutinous texture very soon after cooking.

Notes

For an entrée we place a pile of these 'chips' criss-cross fashion in the middle of a plate, with a pool of the sauce to one side, and dust the plate with very finely chopped pistachios for that extra 'theatre on the plate'.

A garnish of thinly sliced orange, roasted in the oven to enrich and darken and piled to one side of the sauce, also goes down very well. Like most produce that is roasted, the flavour of the oranges is intensified. Try roasting fresh peach, sugared mulberries and even kiwifruit.

Herbed Rabbit Clafoutis *with* Fresh Grape Chutney

Clafoutis is traditionally a cake of black cherries, ideally wild ones, sunk in a sweetened batter which may also be flavoured with rum or Cognac. A savoury clafoutis is not unusual but the use of rabbit is. This dish is a little like a Yorkshire pudding in texture, and goes very well with the fresh grape chutney.

I enjoy the light gamey flavours of rabbit, and find that in this combination no one flavour seems to dominate. Rabbit is a very mild meat, not unlike free-range chicken, and I find it glorious as an entrée.

I was dragged over the coals by a food critic once for serving this on Bunnykins nursery plates. I thought the combination of such a classically presented dish on a fun plate would be wonderful. Perhaps the fact that we said 'Peter Pie' as we put it down did not help!

2 cups cooked rabbit meat
½ teaspoon freshly cracked white pepper
3 spring onions, finely chopped
1 tablespoon olive oil
1 tablespoon butter
2 small onions, finely chopped
2 cloves garlic, crushed
2 red peppers, seeded and diced into 1 cm pieces
2 cups milk
1 cup cream
½ cup flour
½ teaspoon hot pepper sauce
¾ teaspoon salt
4 eggs
2 tablespoons finely chopped herbs

Herbed *Rabbit* Clafoutis

Preheat the oven to 180°C/350°F. Lightly grease an earthenware baking dish, flan dish or individual gratin dishes.

If you are cooking rabbit meat especially for this dish, poach it very lightly in chicken stock, leave it to cool in the stock then slice across the grain quite finely. Proceed as per the rest of the recipe. If you are using already cooked rabbit, the meat can be angle sliced or simply shredded. The look will differ but the flavour will still be there.

Combine the rabbit meat, white pepper and spring onion with the oil and leave to sit for 2 hours.

Sauté the onion in the butter with the crushed garlic until the onion is soft. Turn up the heat and add the peppers; cook for 2 minutes. Remove from the heat and toss in the rabbit mixture. Pack this mixture into buttered dishes, or one dish.

Place the milk and cream in a saucepan and bring slowly to the boil. When it has boiled pour the liquid over the sifted flour and whisk until cool and lump free. Add the hot pepper sauce and season with salt. Allow the mixture to cool then whisk in the eggs one at a time. Pour the mixture over the rabbit and bake for 30 minutes, or until it is firm and beginning to go golden-brown on top. Remember the smaller the dish, the shorter the cooking time. Dust with finely chopped herbs and serve warm, accompanied with fresh grape chutney.

Fresh Grape Chutney

500 g (1 lb) onions, finely chopped
2 cups water
500 g (1 lb) apples, cored, peeled and diced
4 cups grapes
1 cup water
¾ cup red wine vinegar
¾ cup firmly packed brown sugar
½ teaspoon freshly ground black pepper
salt to taste

Braise-deglaze the finely chopped onions in 2 cups of water until they are a good dark brown. By braise-deglaze I mean cook the onions with no butter or oil until they begin to catch on the bottom, add a little water to deglaze the bottom of the pan, and continue this process until the onions are coloured and all the water has been absorbed.

Add all the other ingredients, cover and simmer for about 10 minutes, until the grapes begin to split. Remove the lid and cook until the mixture is thick, stirring frequently to prevent scorching. Add salt to taste.

Notes

This chutney is best made a few days in advance. It can be frozen but it holds well in the refrigerator for some time. A splash of port gives the chutney a wonderful lift.

Fresh grape chutney goes well with the rabbit, but it is also wonderful on herb toast with thinly sliced smoked pork as a finger food. We fold the chutney into terrines, use it to enrich sauces and combine it with toasted almonds to fill a breast of chicken. I enrich it with marsala, heat it with chicken stock and a splash of cream, pass it through a sieve and create an excellent sauce to go with shank of turkey.

Terrine *of* New Potato, Thyme *and* Double-Cream Brie *with a* Water Vinaigrette

10 small new potatoes
90 g (3 oz) clarified butter
4 tablespoons olive oil
4 apples, preferably granny smith
750 g (1½ lb) double-cream brie
4 tablespoons finely chopped fresh thyme
Maldon salt
freshly ground white pepper

The flavour of double-cream brie brings back to me all the memories of two weeks in Paris. A group of friends and I had a hamper of goodies from a local delicatessen and went off to explore Versailles. I still remember the smell, flavour and texture of that brie, the crisp French bread, smoked quail pâté and the softest red wine I can recall. I cannot for the life of me recall much about Versailles — not that it wasn't great, it's just that the hamper was so perfect.

This is an entrée for the person who likes to entertain but does not like cooking. It is time consuming but can be prepared a few days in advance, brought to room temperature and served. The tartness of the green apples, creaminess of the brie and the woody flavour of the sautéed potatoes create a well-balanced terrine. Fresh thyme can only improve the finished dish and the water vinaigrette is delicate enough not to override any one flavour.

Serve it at room temperature, accompanied by a very light sprinkling of sea salt and freshly ground white pepper.

Method

Preheat the oven to 180°C/350°F. Boil the potatoes in lightly salted water until almost cooked. Cool slightly, remove the skins and slice about 1 cm (½ in) thick. In a sauté pan heat some of the clarified butter and oil mixed together, and sauté the potato until it is golden brown on the edges. Remove the potatoes to kitchen towels to drain. Core and thinly slice the apples (leaving the skins on for colour in the terrine). Sauté in the remaining butter and oil mixture until lightly coloured and softened but still firm. Remove from the pan and leave to drain on a kitchen towel. Slice the brie as thinly as

EXTRAORDINARY ENTRÉES

possible, chilling it a little if it is too soft to work with. This is an exceptional recipe for leftover ends of brie and brie that is too young or too old.

Line the inside of a terrine with baking paper. On the bottom place a layer of apple, arranging it nicely and using the best pieces, as this will be the top when the terrine is turned out. Add a layer of brie, dust with some thyme and a very light dusting of Maldon salt and white pepper. Add a thin layer of potato, dust again with the thyme and seasoning, add a layer of apple and so on until the terrine is filled to 1 cm (½ in) above the top. Cover the top with an oiled piece of tinfoil and seal well.

Place the terrine in a roasting pan and pour in warm water to half-way up the tin. Bake in the oven for 15 minutes, remove, and chill, preferably overnight. Place a weight on top of the terrine to give you a good firm composition. I use a brick wrapped in foil but a jar of fruit or a heavy frypan would do.

Turn the terrine out and slice it very finely. Pour 2 tablespoons of water vinaigrette onto each plate and lay the terrine on top. Dust with cracked pepper and use fresh thyme and apple zest for decoration.

Water *Vinaigrette*

Combine all the ingredients in a bowl, being careful not to mix too briskly or the marbled effect we want will be lost.

4 tablespoons extra virgin olive oil
2 tablespoons rice-wine vinegar
1 tablespoon apple juice
1 tablespoon water
½ tablespoon finely chopped fresh thyme leaves
salt and pepper to taste

Red Wine Confit *with* Green Garlic Soufflé

A confit is really a preservation technique whereby meats are salted to draw out their juices, then gently cooked in rendered fat, and finally put into storage in a bath of the same fat. In modern cookspeak confit has come to refer to anything — meat, vegetable or fruit — that is slowly cooked in oil, butter or perhaps duck fat. It is found on innovative menus throughout the world, for example as a Spanish onion confit, or caramelised red capsicum and balsamic confit, or even one with shallot, walnut and fennel.

With its warming winter flavours and deep aromas, this entrée is delicious and satisfying. I could see it being served as a main course with a salad to follow. But this combination of shallots, walnuts, sun-dried tomatoes and red wine is rich — a little goes a long way. When it is made with really fresh ingredients you'll swear the vegetables have been macerated for hours in port and walnut oil. It makes an excellent entrée followed by a game course.

Baby garlic provides the softest flavoured soufflé you could imagine. The alternative would be to roast heads of garlic, squeeze out the roasted cloves and substitute those for the green garlic. This is a very forgiving dish which does not require great soufflé-making skills, but like all soufflés, it waits for no one when it is ready to be served.

At its most basic the soufflé is a cream sauce into which beaten egg whites are folded. You can make the sauce well in advance, beat the egg whites just before folding in and from here they will wait for about 20 minutes in the fridge before you pop the soufflé into the oven. Always butter and flour the mould to guarantee a good rise. If you are making one large soufflé always serve from the middle of the soufflé and not the edge; to serve from the edge will cause the soufflé to sink. When entertaining more than four guests I find it easier to make individual soufflés.

I like to make these soufflés in small terracotta flowerpots, first filling the water hole up with mashed potato or the like. The pots are well buttered, dusted with parmesan, with perhaps some herbs and toasted breadcrumbs to give a more crunchy side. I have the red wine confit already in the base and I make up the soufflé in total and put the entire dish in the refrigerator before the guests arrive. I preheat the oven, the plates are in the warming drawer and the first course is ready for action. Sometimes I serve this with a small green salad, and in that case the plates are out on the bench, a small undressed salad on each plate and a dressing ready to splash on just as the soufflés are cooked to perfection.

Red Wine *Confit*

30 g (1 oz) butter
12 small shallots, skinned but left whole
12 baby onions, peeled
12 freshly cracked walnut halves
2 sun-dried tomatoes
12 oven-dried olives
1 cup red wine
1 tablespoon sugar
6–8 tomatoes, skinned, seeded and cut into quarters
1 tablespoon coarsely chopped green fennel
sea salt and freshly ground black pepper to taste

Place the butter in a sauté pan and gently cook the shallots and onions until they are lightly coloured. Add the walnut halves, sun-dried tomatoes, olives, red wine and sugar. Cook gently, taking care not to let the mixture catch on the base. A small amount of water or wine may be needed to prevent catching. Once all is cooked, and lightly caramelised (about 30 minutes) add the fresh tomato and fennel, and season. The confit should not be liquid at all but should have a rich, glazed texture.

Green Garlic *Soufflé*

Preheat the oven to 190°C/375°F. To make the soufflé base melt the butter, add the flour and cook the roux for about 2 minutes, being careful not to allow it to colour. Gradually add the milk, yoghurt, finely chopped garlic and thyme. Remove from the heat and fold in the gruyère, 2 tablespoons of the parmesan and the egg yolks. Season with sea salt and freshly ground white pepper. The base can be made to this stage and stored in the fridge for up to 5 days.

Lightly butter 6 ramekins or flowerpots, or one large soufflé dish. Dust with parmesan, using about 2 tablespoons. Whisk the egg whites into soft peaks and fold gently into the soufflé base. Divide the red wine confit between the 6 ramekins, or put it into the large soufflé dish. Spoon the soufflé on top, sprinkle on the remaining parmesan and cook in the oven for 10–12 minutes if small ramekins, 20–25 minutes if one large dish. Serve immediately.

90 g (3 oz) butter
90 g (3 oz) flour
1 cup milk
¼ cup yoghurt
20 young green garlic bulbs, or 15 roasted cloves of garlic, finely chopped
¼ teaspoon finely chopped thyme
¾ cup grated gruyère
5 tablespoons freshly grated parmesan
sea salt and freshly ground white pepper
4 eggs, separated

Notes

The reason for the light roux in this dish is to have the flour well cooked but not flavoured. A nut-brown roux is exactly that, nutty and well-flavoured, and when I am creating a dish that needs a sauce to hold well, to have substance and to add character to the dish, then a nut-brown roux is perfect. In this case we simply want the good honest mellow flavour of the garlic and cheese to come through.

If we were to have a roasted garlic soufflé, with a generous amount of garlic to go on top of hot peppered rare beef, a nut-brown roux base for the soufflé would be magical. It would marry the flavour of the roasted garlic with the beef to perfection.

Garlic has the most wonderful flavour and roasting it gives a rich but mellow, inoffensive quality that will not blow your breath into next week. Simply take whole cloves of garlic, cut off a small slice of the base to expose the garlic cloves, dip in oil, sprinkle with salt and roast, cut side down, in a moderate oven until well coloured — about 20 minutes. The garlic can be served whole or can be squeezed from the cloves and added to sauces, butters or breads as you desire. Garlic bread served piping hot with cloves of garlic placed to one side for guests to scrape out and spread over the bread is heaven, and we often serve whole cloves of garlic to one side of a marinated garlic steak with cracked peppercorns and fresh herbs.

The red wine confit must be well flavoured so do check your seasoning. The soufflé base must also have good flavour as the egg whites will reduce the flavour as they are folded through.

Toasted Ravioli *with* Tomato Rosemary Sauce

This is an entrée with a moist inside, crisp hot outside, and a sauce that has the softness of young rosemary and the richness of good tomatoes. A lovely summer entrée.

By dipping the ravioli into the flour and egg and then into parmesan and breadcrumbs you get a crisp nutty outside. It is important to have good hot oil, not overcrowd the pot and drain the ravioli well once it is cooked.

We have served these crisp ravioli piled into a large soup bowl and drizzled with extra virgin olive oil, accompanied with bowls of shaved parmesan — a simple but effective combination for a light luncheon, a beginning to an Italian feast, or a great entrée perhaps followed by poached beef in broth.

If I have been unable to make the ravioli in time I often make the pasta, roll it out and pull it into small uneven pieces. This we refer to as 'pasta rags'; it's a great trick to use up leftover pasta. We then dip the pasta rags in the egg and parmesan and deep-fry them just the same as the ravioli. Piled onto the middle of a large pasta platter and drizzled generously with the fresh tomato and rosemary sauce, they look magical and have a great flavour to boot. Serve with large bowls of freshly shaved parmesan, some capers soaked to remove their salt and oven-roasted sugared tomatoes. A fun presentation for a simple dish.

Toasted Ravioli

In a small bowl combine the crème fraîche (see Basics), goat's cheese, herbs and lightly beaten egg. Season with salt and pepper, taking into account the strength of the goat's cheese and being careful not to add too much salt. Add a few soft white breadcrumbs if too wet.

Lay half the wonton wrappers out on a bench, brush with water and put a teaspoon of the cheese mixture on each. Lay the remaining wonton wrappers on top and press down. Cut away the excess edges and chill.

Combine the toasted breadcrumbs and parmesan. Dip each ravioli in flour then egg and toss in the breadcrumb and cheese mixture to cover completely.

Heat the oil to 180°C/350°F in a deep-fryer. Drop the ravioli into the oil a few at a time, and fry for 2 minutes, or until golden. Drain on paper towels. Serve hot with Tomato Rosemary Sauce.

1 cup crème fraîche
½ cup goat's cheese
2 tablespoons finely chopped herbs
1 egg, lightly beaten
salt and freshly ground black pepper
soft white breadcrumbs (optional)
1 packet (50) wonton wrappers
1 cup toasted breadcrumbs
½ cup parmesan, freshly grated
½ cup flour
1 egg, lightly beaten
4 cups oil

EXTRAORDINARY ENTRÉES

1 tablespoon olive oil
250 g (½ lb) skinned tomatoes or canned Italian plum tomatoes (chopped)
1 teaspoon minced garlic
pinch of red pepper flakes or cayenne
1 tablespoon tomato paste
¼ teaspoon finely chopped fresh rosemary
½ teaspoon sugar
salt and pepper to taste
2 tablespoons chopped parsley

Tomato *Rosemary* Sauce

Heat the olive oil in a sauté pan over low heat. Add the tomato, garlic and red pepper flakes. Raise the heat and sauté for 10 minutes. Add the tomato paste, rosemary, sugar and seasoning. Simmer for 10 more minutes. Remove from the heat and stir in the parsley. Serve at room temperature.

Deep-frying

When deep-frying, always make sure you preheat the oil to 170° or 180°C/350°F. This will ensure that the food is sealed the minute it's added and the amount of oil soaked up will be minimal. The cardinal rule is always to drain the food well on a generous pile of clean paper towels.

A frying thermometer is a cheap and worthwhile investment when frying at home. It clips onto the side of the pot and instantly tells you the temperature of the oil.

Avocado *and* Sugar-Cured Bacon Wrapped *in* Yoghurt Pastry

The flavours in this dish are very simple, yet everyone loves it. I first made this for an impromptu dinner party some eight years ago and although I have lightened the sauce, the dish basically remains the same. Hot avocado is one of my most wicked loves. But overcook avocado and it will be bitter. Make the dish up in total, chill it well and put it in the oven just long enough to cook the pastry to a crisp and no more — perfect.

Sugar-cured bacon has a delicious full malty taste that goes well with the flavour of avocado. My grandfather would salt the freshly cut bacon, leave it for two days, wash it, then rub into the meat a mixture of salt, saltpetre, brown sugar and black pepper with a hint of allspice. The bacon was turned every day and finally would hang for 24 hours up the chimney of the open fire in the living room. I can remember this bacon hanging in the old stables for weeks on end, and my grandmother would simply slice it off as she needed it.

A Danish bacon, preferably unsteamed, would be fine. By unsteamed, I refer to the modern practice of half-cooking bacon to make it easier to slice thinly, a practice that I feel removes a lot of the flavour. Bacon cured by an old-fashioned butcher has a glorious flavour — track down a source for future use.

The use of walnut butter from the éclair appetiser shows how easily one can chop and change recipes. The sauce with leeks and walnuts is luxurious, but will turn the most insipid purple-grey if overheated. Sounds complicated? It's not, but you do need to be very

EXTRAORDINARY ENTRÉES

careful with the timing. Once made up and wrapped in pastry the avocados will hold in the fridge for several days; the addition of lemon juice and the fact that they are virtually airtight helps them keep well.

Yoghurt Pastry

Put the yoghurt, butter and flour into a bowl, add a pinch of salt and knead the ingredients to a firm dough. Wrap the dough in plastic and put it in the refrigerator to rest for 30 minutes.

Dust the bench very lightly with flour and roll the pastry out very thinly. Put it back in the refrigerator while you complete the next stage.

125 g (4 oz) yoghurt, at room temperature
125 g (4 oz) butter, at room temperature
300 g (10 oz) flour
pinch of salt

Avocado and Sugar-Cured Bacon

Preheat the oven to 180°C/350°F. Halve the avocados, remove the stones and skin. Rub lightly with lemon juice and wrap 1 rasher of bacon around each half. Chill for 5 minutes then place in a moderate oven for 2 minutes to firm up the bacon and adhere it to the avocado. Remove from the oven and chill again.

Combine the walnuts, breadcrumbs, softened butter, thyme and seasonings. Add more breadcrumbs as needed to make a good pâté texture and check that it is well seasoned. Fill the cavity of the avocado with the walnut pâté, pulling back the bacon if necessary to make room.

Brush the bacon with a light egg glaze. Roll out the pastry and cut into thin strips. Carefully wrap the pastry around the avocado and bacon, pastry-horn fashion, so the finished avocado is wrapped in pastry and looks a little like a snail. Brush again with the egg glaze, being careful not to let the egg wash run as this could ruin the look. Chill well then bake for 15 minutes, until coloured a light nut-brown.

3 avocados
6 rashers good smoky bacon
juice of 1 lemon
½ cup chopped, lightly toasted walnuts
½ cup toasted brown bread-crumbs
100 g (4 oz) butter, softened
1 teaspoon chopped fresh thyme
sea salt and freshly ground black pepper
1 egg mixed with a pinch of salt for glaze
yoghurt pastry

Leek and Walnut Sauce

Put the white wine and stock in a small saucepan. Add the onion and leek and cook for 10 minutes. Purée and pass through a sieve. Put back into the clean saucepan and whisk in the cream and egg yolks over gentle heat, taking care not to bring the mixture to the boil. Add the walnuts just before serving to prevent discolouring.

Often when I am caught short for an entrée, I simply fill half an avocado generously with walnut butter, brush it with French dressing and bake in the oven uncovered but sitting up to hold the butter. It's very fattening, far too buttery, and loved by all.

125 ml (4 fl oz) white wine
300 ml (10 fl oz) chicken stock
1 small onion, finely chopped
2 leeks, white part only, washed and finely chopped
150 ml (5 fl oz) cream
2 egg yolks
60 g (2 oz) finely chopped walnuts

Galette *of* Leek *with* Fig Tapenade *and* Salad *of* Lamb Shoulder

6–8 leeks, washed and cut into 1.5 cm (¾ in) pieces and steamed
thinly sliced roasted lamb shoulder

Lamb shoulder is one of the firmest and most glutinous of lamb cuts, yet it is tender enough for grilling or roasting over high heat. I enjoy the flavour of this cut of meat, and as in this recipe I like to roast it, basting it well, and serve it chilled, thinly sliced and tossed with a herb vinaigrette. What could be more banal and commonplace than roast lamb? But tossed with the vinaigrette and served on the galette of leek, the flavour is a joy.

This is a fragrant and not insubstantial first course, which may be prepared as individual galettes for an elegant dinner party or as one large tart for a more homely presentation.

Galette Pastry

1½ cups all-purpose flour, chilled in freezer
pinch of salt
125 g (4 oz) butter, very cold
½ cup iced water
salt and finely ground pepper

Place the flour and salt on a cold work surface. Cut the butter into 1 cm (½ in) pieces. With a pastry scraper, cut the butter into the flour until half is the size of peas and the other half a little larger than that. Add all of the water and mix until the pastry forms a ball.

Alternatively this pastry can be made in an electric mixer, adding the butter in stages but the water still all at once. Roll the dough on a well-floured surface into a 40 cm (15 in) circle.

Fig *Tapenade*

3 sprigs rosemary
1 cup olive oil
¾ cup reconstituted dried figs
1 cup kalamata olives, pitted
2 tablespoons capers
10 anchovy fillets
4–5 tablespoons lemon juice
salt and pepper

Fry the rosemary sprigs in a little of the oil. Remove the rosemary and set it aside. Cool the rosemary-infused oil then add it to the balance of the oil. Top and tail the dried figs and cut them into small pieces. Process the figs, olives, fried rosemary, capers and anchovies to a purée. Season with lemon juice, salt and pepper. Pour in the olive oil slowly as if making a mayonnaise.

Notes

The leeks must be young and small.

The fig tapenade can be made weeks in advance if wished, but the finished galette should come straight from the oven to the table to capture all the aroma.

The lamb could be left over from a previous meal, but it should be moist, cooked barely to medium, and still retain a soft pink colour. Remember that the vinaigrette will 'cook' the meat, so for perfect colour toss just prior to serving. If the meat has been cooked longer than is ideal then leave it to soak up the parsley dressing and add some extra olive oil to be absorbed. Season well.

Lamb *Dressing* with Parsley

Combine the garlic and the first measure of olive oil and leave for at least 30 minutes.

To make the vinaigrette, combine both the remaining measures of olive oil and add the lemon juice and champagne vinegar, whisking together. Add the garlic and oil mixture. Taste, season as needed with salt and freshly ground pepper, and add the parsley.

To finish and serve, preheat the oven to 180°C/350°F. Roll the pastry out and spread the tapenade over, place the leeks on top and pull in the edges so that they slightly overlap the leeks. Place the galette on an oven tray and bake for 35–40 minutes, until golden brown. Remove from the oven and after 5 minutes slide the galette off the pan and onto a cooling rack. Rest the galette and while it is still warm pile on the thinly sliced lamb that has been tossed in the dressing.

1 clove garlic, very finely chopped
1 tablespoon olive oil
3 tablespoons extra virgin olive oil
3 tablespoons olive oil
1½ tablespoons lemon juice
1 teaspoon champagne vinegar or rice wine vinegar
salt and freshly ground pepper
½ cup parsley, finely chopped

Coriander Tuiles *with* Pickled Scallops

This is a supremely adaptable recipe, the components of which may be transformed into many guises to be used in a variety of ways.

Tuiles are the most wonderful crisp biscuits; these savoury ones are a little different, great as an accompaniment to delicious pickled scallops but also excellent on their own.

Unlike most tuile recipes, you do need to spread these out very thinly with a fork on the tray as the heat does not make them move. They must be almost lacy thin and lightly golden when cooked. A tuile can never be too thin. As soon as they are out of the oven place them over a cup, a broom handle or a wooden spoon so they firm to the shape you desire. Store them in airtight containers and they will last for up to 2 weeks; freeze them and you will have perfect tuiles available for the next two months. They are always best, however, made the afternoon of the day they are needed.

This recipe makes 25.

Coriander *Tuiles*

3 cloves garlic
8 tablespoons soft butter
2 tablespoons sugar
¾ teaspoon salt
2 egg whites
1 small chilli, finely chopped
1 tablespoon chopped coriander
1 tablespoon chopped mint
8 tablespoons plain flour
4 tablespoons finely grated parmesan

Preheat the oven to 200°C/400°F. Boil the garlic in water for 10 minutes. Drain and mash with a fork. Cream the butter and sugar, add the salt, egg white and mashed garlic. Beat until well combined.

Fold in the chilli, coriander, mint, flour and parmesan. Rest the mixture in the fridge for at least half an hour, then place teaspoons of the mixture onto greased trays. Flatten with the back of a fork dipped in cold water. Bake for 6–8 minutes. Remove from the oven and immediately place each tuile over the handle of a wooden spoon, or whatever will give you the desired shape. Cool on a rack.

Pickled Scallops

500 g (1 lb) fresh scallops
½ cup plain flour
150 ml (¼ pint) olive oil
1 carrot, peeled and cut into julienne strips
1 lemon, thinly sliced
1 onion, thinly sliced
300 ml (½ pint) white wine vinegar
3 fresh bayleaves, roughly chopped
1 clove garlic, peeled and crushed
2 teaspoons sea salt
½ teaspoon freshly ground white pepper
¼ cup water

IN A SMALL MUSLIN BAG PUT:
3 dried chillies
1 teaspoon whole cloves
2 teaspoons whole allspice
7 cm (3 in) stick of cinnamon

Dry the scallops, lightly toss them in the flour and shake off the excess. I sit them in a sieve and give it a few gentle shakes to remove the spare flour. Heat a little oil in a frypan and over a good fierce heat quickly sauté the scallops so that they are well coloured but not cooked.

Put the scallops into a shallow container so that they cool down quickly. Toss through the julienne of carrot and lay the thinly sliced lemon on top.

Heat the remaining oil in a small pan and cook the onion for about 5 minutes. Add all the remaining ingredients, including the muslin spice bag, and simmer for 15

minutes. You may need to add water if the solution is too strong. Pour the solution over the scallops and leave for a few hours to work.

Nelson scallops are just right after 2 hours, but Queen scallops will take only $1\frac{1}{2}$ hours.

Any leftover solution can be stored and drizzled over freshly grilled seafood to give you an 'instant pickle'. Few entrées could be as simple and satisfying as a quick sauté of seafood, cooked to colour, tossed with this vinaigrette and served with slices of rye bread spread with salted butter, and a glass of chilled white wine.

If you are using large pieces of firm fish leave it in the solution with the spice bag for at least 24 hours.

Notes

Try the coriander tuiles with pâtés, salsa, or simply on their own in large bowls for pre-dinner nibbles. They are wonderful with chilli beef, with gazpacho mayonnaise, as an accompaniment to a salad of roasted tomato, and they are delicious with a simple homemade chutney.

Using mint only (without coriander), serve the tuiles as an accompaniment to potted lamb, or add some orange and serve them with duck and wild-rice salad.

When I am pickling scallops I much prefer the large Nelson scallops with their bright red coral attached. They are large, milky and have the most delicious, fragrant flavour. However, I have also made this dish at a friend's home in Paris and used petoncles, tiny French scallops, and found the recipe worked just as well. Just remember the smaller the scallop the shorter the time they can stay in the pickle as it may 'overcook' them. Play around a little to come up with the strength of solution you prefer for your scallops, and remember that like most seafood, scallops are better undercooked than overdone. Queen scallops are fine, but as they are tiny I find $1\frac{1}{2}$ hours is all they need in the solution.

Escalopes of firm white fish are also suitable for this recipe. The fish can stay in the pickle for up to four days, and for a luncheon we serve the fish on herbed croûtons with a julienne salad piled on top and aïoli to finish. The combination looks and tastes glorious. The fish is sautéed first so that it is the lightest brown colour, and we make the croûtons from sourdough bread fried in herb-infused oil and finished in the oven to give a good crisp croûton.

Try and marry the flavours together when making croûtons, and make sure they have very little oil content. Always sauté them quickly and finish them in the oven so that they are crisp and any excess oil is removed. Croûtons made this way will store well in an airtight container.

Do not use a nut oil unless you are going to eat the croûtons within the next day or so as they are inclined to become rancid very fast. Walnut oil becomes rancid most quickly, and it is best kept in the fridge.

Butter on croûtons is fine, but go very lightly. It is best to melt the butter, season it well and brush it lightly over the bread, then bake the croûtons until golden. These need to be stored in the freezer if you intend to keep them for any length of time.

stunning Sorbets & sump

Black Grape and Cardamom Sorbet 85
Grapefruit and Tequila Sorbet 86
Seafood Salad with Citrus Sorbet 87
Duck and Wild Rice Salad with Roasted Oranges 88
Salad of Chicken with Tamarillo 90
Hot Salad of Beef with Basil 91
Turban of Two Salmon with Gazpacho Dressing 92
Salad of Tomato, Roasted Garlic, Shallots and White Truffle Oil 94
Cathedral Salad of Herbs with Champagne Dressing and Witloof 96
Salad of Rare Beef with Pickled Walnuts and Horseradish 98
Salad of Camembert with Mint, Peach and Ginger 100

uous *Salads*

W*hether* you serve a salad or sorbet as a pre-dinner course, as an intermezzo or as the main event, the choice is unlimited. The aim is to come up with a course that matches the occasion. The colours, textures and pungencies of the salad, the bite, crispness and ultimate flavour of the sorbet, all go to create the touches that make up your individual style.

Perhaps it is because of my love of Persian food that I find the sorbet so fascinating. In Persia it was called 'sharbah', which later became 'sorbet' in French and 'sherbet' in English. Honey and fruit juices chilled with snow was one of the most popular early forms of sorbet. Today we have developed these to such heights as Sorbet au Sauternes et au Stilton of Madeleine Kammon fame — one of my favourite combinations.

Sorbets are basically mixtures of fruit juice, coffee, champagne or puréed fruit with either a simple sugar and water syrup or just sugar. While egg white is sometimes added to make the sorbet creamier I find that it removes so much of the flavour that in general it is of little value. However, in the black grape and cardamom sorbet the white stops the sorbet setting like a rock and the cardamom flavour is strong enough to cope.

I make all my sorbets in roasting trays and put them in the freezer, pulling them out once they are frozen, beating them again and freezing them once more. I remove the sorbet about five minutes before serving it.

When dealing with sorbet ingredients, do not use a carbon steel knife for cutting as the acid reacts with the metal and produces a metallic taste throughout the sorbet. I find it best to avoid tin and carbon steel totally.

Like a salad, your sorbet will only be as good as its individual components and, again just as in a salad, the beauty is in its taste and texture. The combinations are endless, but freshness is the vital ingredient.

It is important to think about the ingredients when making sorbet. Some fruit, such as the grapefruit in the grapefruit and tequila sorbet, have a high acid content, while others such as the gooseberry are lower in acid. The acidity of the fruit affects the sugar content and hence the freezing times and consistency. The higher the acid, the more sugar is needed. Remember, too, that not enough acid and the flavour may not be as good. Sometimes a squeeze of lemon or lime is required to accentuate the flavour of the fruit.

STUNNING SORBETS & SUMPTUOUS SALADS

I recall being so pleased with myself when I first served the seafood salad with citrus sorbet, and similarly when I combined freshly picked peaches with camembert, tomato and mint and created the most delightful small appetiser salad which we served on a little peach leaf. The black grape and cardamom sorbet was developed from plump, overripe black grapes that were in abundance from the massive grapevines that grew in my mother's garden.

I relish the sorbet and salad courses. A crisp, well-flavoured sorbet, whether it is the 'entrement', served between the first and the main courses, the accompaniment to an entrée, or a light dessert, is simple and satisfying. A salad can be treated in much the same way within a menu; the French squeeze it in between the meat and cheese courses, in California it is eaten at lunch, dinner and, given the choice, I am sure these diet-conscious Americans would have it at breakfast as well. Here in the Antipodes, we most often have a green salad with the main course as a light luncheon, and a 'salade composée' as a first course; very rarely do we consider the salad as an intermezzo course.

'I have *enthusiasm*, I've read a lot *and* studied with *other* chefs, but mine is a trial and error *approach*.'

The modern salad is a feast of colour, texture and taste. As new and exotic salad leaves have become increasingly available we have learned to create mesclun salads with such greens and herbs as the curly green and red batavia, purple radicchio, and greenish and brown oakleaf lettuces. The radicchio has a slightly bitter taste, the curly endive is more subtle, whereas the oakleaf has a delicate, sweetish taste, and the lamb's lettuce or mache is slightly more elusive. Sage, dill and tarragon are often added, and bitter dandelion greens and arugula give a bite. Whatever the combination, the salad green must be the freshest and the crispest your garden or the market can provide.

In this section, however, I am looking at more substantial salads. I believe a salad is a way of emptying your refrigerator, and I encourage you to try different combinations. I am certainly not saying that a salad is a dumping trough for all your stale leftovers; a salad is a way to use fresh, healthful ingredients interestingly, to create a luxurious dish with colours, textures and flavours that complement each other.

Leftover beef could be used to create the rare-beef salad with pickled walnut mousse and horseradish cream; cheese that has aged could be tossed with the

tomato and mint combination, and a generous supply of grapefruit could be combined with avocado and honey to give you a superb entrée salad. Spare herbs could be gently washed, dried and tossed with champagne vinaigrette, and served as an accompaniment to tajine of chicken.

To get the most from your salads there are a few pointers that should always be taken into account. Any greens should be washed and well dried, otherwise the leaves will be limp and soggy. The components for all salads can be prepared in advance but mixed just prior to serving, and when dressing a salad always err on the light side. With the exception of tomatoes, most salad ingredients should be served at room temperature where the textures and flavours are most pronounced and perfumes blend more readily. The salad of camembert, tomato and mint with fresh peach is a good example of this, as is the tamarillo and chicken salad. I remove greens from the cooler about 15 minutes before serving so that their true flavours come through.

The ingredients used to dress a salad depend entirely upon the composition of the salad. I prefer vinegar to lemon juice in my dressings as I find lemon can be tart and mean. I like to create yoghurt dressings rather than cream-based salad sauces, and I enjoy experimenting with different oils and vinegars. Roasted hazelnut and walnut oils make nutty additions to a salad, and although olive oil can be a little too pungent for some green leaves, when mixed with a small amount of peanut oil it is perfect. I love sesame oil, but it is easy to overdo the flavours. Champagne vinegar and rice-wine vinegar are delightfully mellow, but I love malt vinegar with vine-ripened tomatoes and shallots. As for balsamic vinegar that has been aged in wooden casks like a fine wine, I much prefer to drink it. The more common varieties of balsamic vinegar are now made in stainless steel vats; they are excellent sprinkled on a salad or used in meat and vegetable marinades.

Black Grape *and* Cardamom Sorbet

This sorbet was born out of the need to make use of an excess of ripe black grapes during a very hot summer. We made the black grape juice by putting oodles of grapes in the blender, and puréeing them to a pulp. Then we hung this in a muslin bag and let the juice drip out. Bought juice is of course perfectly suitable, but check the sugar content and alter the recipe to suit. Serves 4.

Method

Combine the sugar, cardamom and grape juice and stir well so that the sugar dissolves. Bring to the boil and cook for 4 minutes, cool and strain. Pour into a container and freeze for 4 hours, uncovered.

Whisk the egg whites until they form soft peaks. Remove the grape mixture from the freezer and break it up with a spoon. Carefully fold in the egg whites followed by the lemon juice — the mixture should be light and fluffy.

Return the sorbet to the freezer for 3 hours, until it is completely set. Before serving, place the sorbet in the fridge for 15 minutes to make it easier to scoop. Serve decorated with grapes.

30 g (1 oz) castor sugar
6 cardamom pods, crushed
300 ml (½ pint) black grape juice
2 egg whites
1 tablespoon lemon juice
handful of black grapes, to decorate

Grapefruit *and* Tequila Sorbet

I have used this sorbet all over the world, putting it together for friends in Oregon, for a family in Ireland and for fellow chefs in Australia. I have, in fact, built my restaurant on this sorbet. We served it as an intermezzo sorbet for ten years, until it became unfashionable, but regulars still ask for it so a constant supply is always available for those 'in the know'. It's a dazzling sorbet, not only in colour and texture, but also the flavour. Excellent with seafood salad, great as an intermezzo, and just heaven as a refreshing dessert course with perhaps some grapefruit macerated in more tequila and sweetened with honey.

Method

2 cups strained grapefruit juice
juice of 1 lemon
2 tablespoons tequila
2 cups sugar syrup

To make sugar syrup combine sugar and water in the ratio of 1 cup sugar to 2 cups water, boil this, and cool it before drawing off the 2 cups of sugar syrup.

Combine the grapefruit and lemon juice with the tequila and sugar syrup. Freeze overnight. The next day, place the bowl and beaters of a mixer in the freezer for a few minutes. Take the frozen block of juice out, let it sit for 10 minutes, then chop it into large pieces. Beat the mixture quickly to break up any granules and return it to the freezer.

Serve in chilled martini or wine glasses, topped with fresh grapes or perhaps a couple of long slivers of grapefruit peel and a sprig of mint.

Seafood Salad *with* Citrus Sorbet

This dish can be served in combination as presented here, as a light appetiser or entrée at a formal dinner, as a summer luncheon dish, or taken separately in chilled thermos flasks to a smart picnic.

The hint of lemon verbena in the sorbet gives it just that little additional flavour. Remember that a high acid content does slow down the setting, so give yourself plenty of time.

Citrus Sorbet

Gently heat the water and sugar until the sugar has dissolved, then bring to a simmer for 5 minutes. Add the lemon juice and zest, orange juice, lemon verbena and salt. Cool and place in a shallow metal tray. Freeze in the coldest part of your freezer and stir 2 or 3 times during freezing. Once it is frozen rake the sorbet with a fork, pack it into airtight containers and freeze until needed. When made in an ice-cream machine this sorbet has a creamier texture.

¾ cup water
¾ cup sugar
2½ cups fresh lemon juice
zest of 2 lemons, finely chopped
½ cup fresh orange juice, sieved
¼ teaspoon salt
2 teaspoons finely chopped lemon verbena (optional)

Seafood Salad

Buy the freshest seafood you can get. Poach it in water with the white wine, cracked pepper and sea salt, until it is just opaque. Do not let it boil at any time, and keep the liquid for later use. If using mussels poach them last, as they have a strong flavour. Oysters should be left raw. Keep the seafood pleasantly chilled until 15 minutes before serving, then toss with the other ingredients.

To serve, pile about 90 g (3 oz) of the seafood mixture onto each mains-sized plate. Put 2 small quenelles of the sorbet to one side and garnish with lemon verbena. I like to serve this course with small bowls of Maldon salt and generous wedges of meyer lemons, accompanied by a shot of ice-cold vodka.

500 g (1 lb) seafood
1 cup white wine
2 cups water
½ teaspoon cracked pepper
½ teaspoon sea salt
3 tablespoons French dressing (see Basics)
zest of 1 lemon
1 teaspoon coarsely cracked white pepper
2 tablespoons finely chopped herbs (chervil, chives, parsley, tarragon)

Note

The key to this recipe is good fresh seafood, cooked very lightly, and not combined until the very last moment. I find that if I combine scallops with crab, perhaps some prawns, and lightly poached baby mussels, the flavours do not stay honest to themselves and everything mingles into one nondescript seafood flavour. It is pointless to spend time at the markets choosing the freshest available seafood only to overcook it or toss it with other flavours too soon. The aim of a seafood combination is to enjoy each flavour, true to itself; it is not to turn silk purses into sows' ears!

Duck *and* Wild Rice Salad *with* Roasted Oranges

2 cups wild rice
4 tablespoons butter
5 carrots, finely chopped
1 large red onion, finely chopped
1 medium-sized duck that has been cooked in stock and chilled
3 cups stock from the duck (see Notes)
2 oranges, roasted and finely chopped (see Notes)
1 cup lightly toasted pinenuts
1 cup currants, plumped in a splash of white wine
zest of 2 oranges, finely chopped
½ cup finely chopped chives
¼ cup finely chopped fresh thyme
½ cup finely chopped Italian parsley
¾ cup fresh orange juice
olive oil
sea salt and freshly ground black pepper
finely chopped chives for garnish
small bunch of fresh watercress for garnish

This salad may be served as part of a buffet, as a first-course salad, or even on its own as a simple luncheon dish accompanied by crusty homemade bread. Any leftover salad makes a great filling for pita bread, or it can be rolled in the thinnest of crêpes and heated with a light orange glaze.

The list of ingredients in this recipe may look long but it is delightfully simple to create. Add or change any flavours according to your taste — you may like to combine garlic, another herb or just more seasoning. Although the salad may be served right away, it reacts well to a bit of aging.

Method

Preheat the oven to 190°C/375°F. Soak the wild rice in cold water for 1 hour. Drain. Bring a pot of water to the boil and add the rice. Boil for 5 minutes, then drain and set to one side.

In a large frypan melt the butter, or duck fat if you have any. Add the carrot and onion and sauté for 10 minutes, stirring regularly. Add the rice, cooking a few minutes longer.

Transfer the rice to a roasting pan and pour the stock over it. Cover with foil and place in the oven for about 40 minutes, or until the rice is tender and the liquid has been absorbed.

Meanwhile shred all the meat from the duck. Keep the skin separate and bake this again until it is crisp. Finely dice the skin, sprinkle lightly with sea salt and put to one side.

Transfer the cooked rice to a bowl and add the duck meat, roasted orange, pinenuts, currants, orange zest and fresh herbs. Toss to combine and dress the salad with the orange juice, olive oil and if necessary some of the stock from the duck. Season well.

Transfer to a large platter and sprinkle with the crisp skin of the duck, some finely chopped chives and serve. For individual servings, pack the salad into a small cup, turn it out onto the middle of a large white plate, dust the plate with fresh, finely chopped herbs and drizzle some lush green olive oil around the salad. Garnish with watercress.

A salad is best served at room temperature to appreciate the combination of flavours.

Roasting Fruit

To roast oranges, or any other fruit for that matter, slice the fruit, skin and all, into rounds 1 cm (½ in) thick. Spread out in a roasting tray, drizzle with a small amount of olive oil and dust lightly with brown sugar. Bake in a moderate oven until the fruit is well coloured and shrivelled.

Roasted orange slices can be finely chopped and frozen for later use, packed in jars and covered in light olive oil for use in salads or as a seasoning for ragout of beef with orange, or puréed and used in a vinaigrette for such vegetables as beetroot or kumara. The oranges can be left in the oven on a very low temperature all night, then packed dry into large jars, for use in similar ways to glazed fruit.

Roasting fruits gives the most intense flavour and has great scope for use in many dishes — pork with roasted plum garnish and green peppercorns, chicken with roasted peach and Sauternes — just about any fruit can be roasted to intensify the flavour.

Poaching duck for meat and stock

Wash the duck to remove any blood. Put it into a pot slightly larger than the bird, with a sliced onion, bayleaf, some carrot peelings and black peppercorns. Cover with water, bring gently to the boil and salt lightly. I often add the zest from an orange, a few juniper berries and the stalks from some parsley and fresh thyme. I like my stocks to have substance — if I wanted watery stock, I would take it from the tap. The duck will be cooked when the leg moves freely at the joint, probably after 1–1½ hours, depending on the size and age of the bird. Cool the duck and remove all the meat from the bird. Put the bones, skin and any fat that has been removed from the bird back into the stock pot and reduce it by a third. This will give you excellent well-flavoured stock to work with

Duck fat

When cooking duck always keep the fat. Chill the stock and remove the layer of fat from the top. Place the fat in a small pan, bring it to the boil then pour it gently into small containers and freeze. Use it to fry potatoes, instead of butter in game sauces, and for frying onions, caramelising leeks and enriching soups. Duck fat is much lower in cholesterol than butter and has much more flavour.

Duck fat, good stock and fresh herbs are some of my most valued cooking ingredients. Followed perhaps by whole white pepper and good sea salt.

Salad *of* Chicken *with* Tamarillo

meat from 1 medium-sized chicken (see Note)
180 g (6 oz) celery, peeled, thinly sliced and blanched
1 cup hazelnuts, roasted and skinned
8 tamarillos, blanched, peeled and halved
2 tablespoons fresh flat-leaf parsley leaves
¾ cup spiced mayonnaise (see below)

This is a particular favourite among meat salads. When you add hazelnuts and the creamy dressing you have a real eye-opener. Do make the effort to prepare the dressing in advance and let it sit overnight — it is considerably better. If you don't have the suggested assortment of ingredients, play around with similar flavours. Walnuts, black grapes and chicken are terrific together.

Prepare each ingredient and store them separately until you are ready to toss and dress the salad.

Spiced Mayonnaise

¼ cup cream
1 tablespoon lemon juice
6 tablespoons homemade mayonnaise (see Basics)
¼ teaspoon salt
1 tablespoon freshly ground cinnamon
¼ teaspoon ground allspice
1 small clove garlic, crushed with ¼ teaspoon salt
1 tablespoon coriander seeds, finely ground
2 teaspoons sugar
2 tablespoons finely chopped root ginger
½ teaspoon tabasco sauce, or ¼ teaspoon cayenne

Mix all the ingredients together and store in a covered container in the refrigerator. This mayonnaise will keep for several weeks and is an excellent dressing for cold fish, tossed with pickled pork or as a dip for garden-fresh crudités.

Poaching chicken

To bring out the best flavour in the chicken and give you excellent stock, follow this method. Place the chicken in a pot of water, large enough for the bird to be covered. Bring it gently to the boil, removing the scum as it rises, and add to the pot 12 peppercorns, 1 finely diced carrot, 1 finely diced small onion and ½ cup of celery leaves. Add 3 cloves, 3 allspice, a sprig of thyme, 1 chopped clove of garlic and 1 teaspoon of sea salt. Have the water barely trembling and poach until the chicken is just cooked, for about 45 minutes. Take the chicken out of the stock after it has rested in the hot stock for 10 minutes and remove all the meat from the bird, putting the bones, skin and any fat back in the pot. Reduce the liquid to a good stock, pass it through a sieve, chill, and remove the fat. Freeze in quantities that suit your cooking.

To cool chicken rapidly, remove the cooked chicken from the stock, lay it on a cold tray and chill. Chill the stock in shallow trays in the fridge. Once both meat and stock are well chilled combine them to keep the chicken moist. Be careful when chilling stock in a large deep container; often the middle of the liquid is so slow to be chilled that the stock will ferment within a day.

When we freeze chicken meat we always do so in stock; that way the meat remains tender and is deliciously plump and well flavoured when thawed.

Frugal chefs always keep their onion skins, carrot peelings, parsley and thyme stalks, and the white root of celery, along with a few peppery celery leaves. These are all kept in plastic bags in the freezer, and added to stocks, along with the appropriate extra herbs and spices, when they require a well-rounded flavour. I only add spices when the meat needs to have an additional touch to marry it to the sauce. I make a note of any stock that may be spiced on my freezer tag, as this could have a considerable effect on a dish. Spiced stock is most often used in meat sauces or rich winter soups.

STUNNING SORBETS & SUMPTUOUS SALADS

Hot Salad *of* Beef *with* Basil

A lovely, almost mysterious variation on the hot stir-fry; this salad might be considered the king of wok cooking. I enjoy the addition of sesame oil and ginger for although you don't see it mixed in with the red meat, your palate detects the pleasant, rounded flavour. Any leftover salad can be used as a sandwich filling, served cold on a hot potato rosti as a light meal or rolled in lettuce and served as picnic food.

For the best results prepare this dish just before serving. Although the ingredients may look complicated it is exceptionally simple to make. Serve it as a buffet salad, as a main course or as a first-course entrée.

Method

Place the beef in a bowl and add the soy, 1 tablespoon of the rice wine, sesame oil and cornflour. Mix well.

Heat a wok or large frying pan until it is very hot, then pour in 2 tablespoons of the peanut oil. Add the beef and stir-fry for 2 minutes to brown. Remove the beef with a slotted spoon and put it to one side. Wipe out the wok and add the remaining peanut oil, the garlic, ginger and onions, and fry for 1 minute. Add the peppers and after another minute the remaining rice wine, chilli bean sauce, sugar and oyster sauce.

Return the beef to the wok to heat through. Add the basil leaves at the last minute and cook until just wilted. Serve.

500 g (1 lb) lean steak, cut into 1 cm strips
1 tablespoon light soy sauce
3 tablespoons Chinese rice wine
1 teaspoon sesame oil
2 teaspoons cornflour
3 tablespoons peanut oil
4 cloves garlic, finely chopped
2 teaspoons finely chopped fresh ginger
250 g (8 oz) finely sliced onions
1 green pepper, seeded and cut into strips
1 red pepper, seeded and cut into strips
2 teaspoons chilli bean sauce
1 teaspoon sugar
1 tablespoon oyster sauce
2 generous handfuls basil leaves

Turban *of Two* Salmon *with* Gazpacho Dressing

3 fillets salmon, skinned and pin bones removed (see Notes)
6 thin slices hot-smoked salmon
1 tablespoon finely chopped dill
1 teaspoon finely chopped tarragon
1 small onion, finely chopped
sea salt and freshly ground white pepper
2 tablespoons citron oil, or good olive oil
juice of 3 lemons

After a wonderful day in the country at Millbrook, the farm of my close friends Gaye and Graham Johnson, we decided to have some other 'townies' out for dinner and to enjoy a few rounds of tennis and petanque. It was a typical Canterbury summer evening, with a light nor'wester blowing and a late sunset, and it was far too balmy to eat heavy food.

Graham had caught some salmon the day before at the mouth of the Rakaia River, so it was still wonderfully fresh, and I had brought out some hot-smoked salmon for everyone to try with drinks. As Graham skinned and boned the fish we discussed what to do with it. After about ten minutes we decided to cut the fresh salmon into long fillets, dust it with fresh dill and tarragon from the herb garden, and roll it all turban style with some of the hot-smoked salmon enclosed in the wheel. Grilled on the metal slab of the barbecue, served with a light gazpacho dressing, an absolutely garden-fresh mesclun salad and a classic chardonnay from the farm cellar, it was a tremendous success. Simple food, flavours that are not too complicated, and great friends. What else is life about, other than perhaps winning just one game of petanque?

Method

Slice the salmon lengthwise so that you have 6 long strips of salmon in total. Lay a slice of hot-smoked salmon on each and divide the dill, tarragon and finely chopped onion between the 6 piles. Season with salt and freshly ground white pepper and roll, securing with a long skewer. Brush each turban with oil and grill over high heat until the fish is barely cooked. We found it took 3 minutes on each side, but this would depend on the grill.

This dish can be cooked in the oven. I would splash some white wine over the turbans, place foil over the salmon and bake for no more than 6 minutes in a moderate oven.

Whichever way you cook the turbans, as soon as they are ready place them on the salad greens and pour a generous spoonful of gazpacho dressing over each. Serve extra dressing to one side.

Notes on skinning salmon

To remove the skin from the salmon fillets, place the fish skin-side down on a cutting board and insert a large knife between the skin and the meat at the tail end. Have a tablespoon of salt to dip your fingers in to give you a good grip of the skin. Cut in a sawing motion, holding onto the edge of the skin and keeping the knife blade slanted down towards the skin.

To remove the pin bones, small bones that you feel in the middle of the fillet as you run your fingers against the grain, use small pliers which grip the bones far better than tweezers. These bones are easier to get out if the fillet is lightly chilled beforehand.

Gazpacho Dressing

Whisk the mayonnaise and pour in the tomato and cucumber juices, adding a little of the water to make a sauce that is of coating consistency. Fold in the rest of the ingredients and correct the seasoning. Cover and chill for at least an hour so that the flavours blend.

2 cups mayonnaise (see Basics)
10–12 vine-ripened tomatoes, puréed and sieved to extract juice
1 large cucumber, seeded, puréed and sieved to extract juice
¼ cup chilled water
2 teaspoons lemon juice
⅛ teaspoon cayenne pepper
sea salt and freshly ground white pepper
a few drops of red-wine vinegar to sharpen

Notes

This dressing is very light, and well flavoured, and is perfect with lightly poached chicken, grilled fish or simply as a sauce for a fresh tomato and red pepper salad. It will keep for two weeks in the fridge.

Thin wedges of apple, sprinkled with vinegar, oil, salt and pepper, are a nice alternative to the mesclun salad as an accompaniment for the salmon.

Salad *of* Tomato, Roasted Garlic, Shallots *and* White Truffle Oil

Make this salad when tomatoes are in season and full of the flavour of sun-ripened fruit. It is an ideal summer salad, bright and full-flavoured. The vinaigrette and the beans may be prepared several hours in advance but do not combine them until the very last minute so the salad will be crisp and fresh tasting. Some palates find the combination of raw garlic and shallots a bit pungent, but roasting them in butter and oil beforehand mellows the flavour beautifully.

Although this is a simple combination of tomato and potato, tossed with the truffle oil it becomes a first-course salad of incredible luxury. Serve it with a sauté of milk-fed lamb in herbs for a light luncheon, pile it onto roast loin of pork for a main course, or serve it as a first course with the lightest dusting of finely chopped chives.

Blanching

For crisp green vegetables such as green beans, blanch in boiling salted water, drain, and plunge directly into iced water for one or two minutes. The colder the bath the better; the cold will stop the cooking and allow the vegetables to retain their bright colour. Do make sure the vegetables are cold the entire way through; if they are taken out of the cold water too soon they will still discolour. Leaving the vegetables in the water too long will waterlog them and they will quickly lose flavour.

STUNNING SORBETS & SUMPTUOUS SALADS

Truffle *Vinaigrette*

1 tablespoon white truffle oil
2 tablespoons virgin olive oil
1 tablespoon sherry vinegar
2 cloves garlic, de-germed (see Note) and finely chopped
1 small onion, finely chopped
sea salt and white pepper to taste

Combine all the ingredients and whisk. If you are making the vinaigrette in advance, keep it in the fridge, bringing it to room temperature 15 minutes before serving.

Salad

Preheat the oven to 180°C/350°F. Scrub the potatoes and place them in a steamer; steam until a skewer or fork comes away easily, 15–20 minutes. While the potatoes are hot, peel them and slice into quarter wedges. Place these in a bowl with the truffle vinaigrette and toss thoroughly. Cover and set aside at room temperature for at least an hour.

Peel the garlic and shallots, taking care to remove any green sprout. Toss the garlic and shallots with the butter and oil and bake until well coloured but not burnt.

Slice the tomatoes into 1 cm (½ in) strips. Blanch and chill the green beans and slice them so that they are no longer than the potato wedges. When you are ready to serve, toss the beans with the parsley and tomato and combine with the potato and vinaigrette, adding the warm garlic and shallots at the last minute.

This salad is so delicate that I prefer to toss it with my hands so I can feel that all the ingredients are well coated and the salad is properly combined. Wooden or plastic salad servers, in my opinion, leave sections of the salad quite untouched by the dressing and often a pool of limp ingredients at the bottom of the bowl.

Check the seasoning and dust lightly with coarse sea salt. Serve in the middle of a warm salad plate with plenty of crusty grilled country-style bread.

10 small potatoes
20 cloves garlic
20 small shallots
1 tablespoon butter
2 tablespoons olive oil
6 vine-ripened tomatoes, peeled and seeded
150 g (5 oz) baby green beans
1 cup Italian broadleaf parsley
coarse sea salt for garnish

Notes

'De-germing' is what you do when you remove any green sprouting from garlic. It is most important otherwise the dish can be very bitter.

Truffle oil is extra virgin olive oil flavoured with truffles. It has a very intense flavour and can be used in pasta sauces, potato purées, risottos and to enrich a dressing. A little truffle oil enhances the flavour of tomatoes, but do be careful as too much will overpower the dish. Often in a dressing we will add drops of the truffle oil to a plain olive oil and check the seasonings from there.

When making this dressing a birch whisk is a great asset. It brings the dressing together into a luxurious creamy consistency in a very short time. An invaluable tool in my kitchen.

To peel tomatoes, cut a criss-cross in the skin on the base of each tomato and cut out the stalk. Immerse the tomatoes in a pan of boiling water for 10 seconds, remove and immerse in iced water. Drain, and their skins will peel off easily.

To remove the seeds from tomatoes a small teaspoon is the best tool. Keep the seeds, dry them out, and use them as a seasoning for pasta, in breads, or as a spiced butter.

Cathedral Salad *of* Herbs *with* Champagne Dressing *and* Witloof

1 cup mixed fresh herb leaves
4 cups small salad greens
4 witloof, leaves separated and chilled

The cathedral salad — so called because when finished it looks like the dome of our local basilica — is very simple and moreish. Witloof is a highly underrated green, and when it is combined with these herbs you have a powerful collaboration. This is a delightful dish to serve with the duo of salmon on a balmy summer evening.

When I was travelling in the United States I was often served the most magical parsley salad. The dressing was simple and the flavour quite sublime. I had it on top of hot grilled steak, on crisp pizza crust, and tossed with hot crusted goat's cheese. It was served on its own in large Mexican bowls as an accompaniment to cold meat, piled on top of a herb broth, and once was even served at a cocktail party rolled in prosciutto, grilled and sitting on a little parsley bread croûton. This recipe is an adaptation of that wonderful parsley salad.

As a cook I adore fresh herbs, and as well as growing them in my own garden at home I have small pots in all my kitchens. They are tended with love, watered, fed and trimmed regularly. At any one time, for at least nine months of the year, we have our own fresh herbs, including sage, tarragon, chervil, parsley, bay, thyme, summer savory, rosemary and chives. Basil is a little more tricky but we harvest it by the sack when it is in season, store it in oil and vinegar or freeze it.

Keep fresh herbs in the refrigerator in a tightly sealed plastic bag. Do not rinse them with water until you use them. Keep the woody stems of your herbs for stocks, for aromatic smoke and to infuse salts.

Champagne Dressing

6 tablespoons olive oil
1½ tablespoons lemon juice
1 teaspoon champagne vinegar
1 tablespoon garlic oil
salt and freshly ground pepper

Wash and dry the herbs and salad greens. Combine the dressing ingredients. In a large, shallow salad bowl combine the herbs and salad greens and toss with your hands. Add some dressing and gently and thoroughly toss until everything is evenly coated.

Place the salad on a plate, toss the witloof in dressing and stand it around the salad, pulling it in at the top so that it totally encases the salad. Brush with extra dressing and sprinkle with some coarsely chopped herbs.

STUNNING SORBETS & SUMPTUOUS SALADS

Notes

As mad as I am about fresh herbs, I do use dried herbs and find the single-minded pursuit of the fresh item for the sake of it, simply in order to say 'I use only fresh herbs', unprofessional. Just as the flavours of wild and domestic mushrooms become concentrated when you dry them, so it is with certain herbs. Dried tarragon in a seafood soup is wonderfully pungent, whereas fresh tarragon in a fish sauce is delicate.

I do not use dried thyme, chives, parsley or rosemary because they are better fresh and are always available, but dried mixed Provençal herbs and dried savory are excellent when obtained from a good supplier. Certainly some dried herbs taste like dust, but fresh herbs badly cooked are just as vile.

When cooking with fresh herbs, be sure to add them to the dish near the end of the cooking time. The fresh taste and colour disappear completely with prolonged cooking. Add dried herbs early in the cooking, to give the heat a chance to release the essential oil. Sometimes a combination of fresh and dried can be sublime; it is worth experimenting with this idea.

In converting a measure for dried herbs to fresh, use at least three times as much of the fresh herb.

Salad *of Rare* Beef *with* Pickled Walnuts *and* Horseradish

What a great marriage — rare beef with a light pickled-walnut mousse spread onto croûtons and served on salad greens with a horseradish cream. It's the best chilled beef salad you're ever likely to encounter. The key here is to cook the beef at a high temperature and chill it fast. The pickled walnut mousse can be made well in advance, but don't spread it on the croûtons until you are ready to serve.

This is the sort of recipe that requires a fair amount of last-minute juggling. You need to keep dancing and to keep your wits about you, but it's certainly worth the effort. What you want to achieve here is a mingling of fresh, specific flavours and the succulence of rare but crusty beef. Finished at the last minute, this dish is a culinary triumph.

Method

500 g (1 lb) fillet steak in 1 piece
1 tablespoon sea salt
1 tablespoon freshly ground black pepper
1 tablespoon finely chopped fresh garlic
2 tablespoons olive oil

Combine the salt, pepper, garlic and oil and mix to a paste. Brush this generously over the fillet steak. Heat a frypan over a fierce heat and sauté the beef until cooked; about 6 minutes on each side gives a rare steak, 10–15 minutes gives medium-rare. This can also be done in a hot oven; I give the fillet 15 minutes in a fierce oven, but it really depends on the thickness of the fillet. Put the cooled steak onto a cold tray and sit it in the fridge to cool down.

Leave the cooked, chilled beef in one piece until you are about to create the salad, then slice the beef into generous 2-cm (¾ in) slices.

Pickled Walnut *Mousse*

250 g (8 oz) cream cheese
½ cup milk
1 tablespoon juice from pickled walnuts
4 spring onions, green and white sections, finely chopped
3–5 pickled walnuts (more if small), finely chopped
1 teaspoon gelatine dissolved in 1 tablespoon water
white pepper and sea salt to taste

Place the cream cheese and milk in a bowl and beat with a wooden spoon to soften. Add the juice of the walnuts, the spring onions and a generous pinch of white pepper. Mix well then gently but thoroughly fold in the finely chopped pickled walnuts and the softened gelatine. You may need more walnuts, depending on the size. Season and store, well covered, in the refrigerator until needed. This will hold for up to 10 days without any problems.

To make the croûtons, bake triangles of white sandwich-slice bread in a slow oven. When cooked and cooled, but not too long before serving, spread generously with the pickled walnut mousse.

Horseradish *Cream*

Mix the first 5 ingredients together, stirring well to dissolve the castor sugar. Slowly add the sour cream. Let the mixture sit for an hour to thicken and improve in flavour. I then thin this down with a drop of water or milk. For this salad the cream needs to be thin enough to dribble on the salad. This mixture holds for a good 10 days in a sealed container in the fridge.

2 tablespoons grated fresh horseradish
1 teaspoon Dijon mustard
2 teaspoons castor sugar
pinch salt
2 tablespoons cider or white-wine vinegar
1 cup sour cream

Salad Greens

6 cups assorted salad greens, washed, dried and loosely packed (preferably a mix of curly endive, radicchio, watercress, lamb's lettuce and arugula)

To assemble the salad, put a cup of salad greens into each of 6 large pasta bowls, tuck in the croûtons of pickled-walnut mousse and the slices of rare beef.

Drizzle over the horseradish cream in a trellis pattern and dust the salad with Maldon salt and cracked pepper for garnish. Long-angled chives look excellent, as does fine julienne of tomato.

An alternative is to slice fillet steak finely, grill it at the last minute and simply toss it hot over the salad just as you serve it.

Cooking rare beef

When we cook rare beef for this salad at Michaels I like to have the meat very rare and moist. To achieve this we first freeze the beef for about half an hour, coat it with the pepper and garlic mixture, and slide it into a very hot oven. Chilling the beef first results in the middle of the fillet remaining very rare. Do not leave the seasoning mixture on the fillet for more than 10 minutes before cooking as the salt will begin to draw out all the liquid, resulting in a dry, tough fillet. I have tried to deep-fry the fillet, which makes the outside wonderfully crunchy, but I dislike the smell of oil so much that I prefer the oven technique.

Salad *of* Camembert *with* Mint, Peach *and* Ginger

Everyone knows what a prince of cheese camembert is. But we also know how cantankerous and temperamental it can be. You serve an excellent camembert when it is ready to be served, not a moment sooner or a minute later. Unfortunately this means that in the restaurant you are often left with camembert which is past its best. Hence we created this salad. Designed especially to make use of a glut of sun-ripened peaches and an overorder of camembert, this salad makes a menu special regardless of whether it is presented as a first course, a main or a cheese course.

I use a 10 cm (4 in) pastry ring to form the salad neatly. If you don't have one of these a clean 180 g (6 oz) tuna can with both ends removed will work beautifully. You can also simply use a spoon and small knife or a spatula.

Ginger Vinaigrette

Whisk all the ingredients together and leave to sit for an hour for the flavours to infuse.

8 cm (3 in) fresh ginger, peeled and finely chopped
6 shallots, finely chopped
75 ml (2.5 fl oz) red wine vinegar
250 ml (8 fl oz) olive oil
juice of 2 lemons
100 ml (4 fl oz) soy sauce
100 ml (4 fl oz) sesame oil
sea salt and freshly ground white pepper

Note

If you squeeze the ginger root and use only its juice, rather than finely chopped or crushed ginger, diners don't need to contend with ginger fibres. Cut the ginger into thin slices and press it into a garlic press over a small glass. Put the fibres into a jar of sherry and use the sherry as an essence to lift the cooking flavours in other dishes.

Salad

Slice the camembert horizontally and then into thin wedges. The peach should be cut to a similar size. Toss the tomato, peach and camembert together with 1 tablespoon of the dressing and add half the mint leaves. Put the pastry ring in the middle of a plate and pat down 3 tablespoons of the salad. Toss the remaining mint with a little dressing and pile it on top of the salad. Remove the ring carefully, pour a little sauce around the salad, and dust the plate with nutmeg.

150 g (5 oz) firm camembert
6 peaches, blanched, peeled, stoned and sliced lengthways
8 tomatoes, peeled, seeded and julienned
½ cup mint leaves, washed, dried and loosely packed
freshly grated nutmeg

Alternative Dressing

This is a creamy alternative dressing for this salad.

Combine all and leave to sit overnight. This dressing can be thinned with water if it is too thick.

1 cup thick mayonnaise (see Basics)
2 cups cream
½ teaspoon freshly grated nutmeg
½ teaspoon sea salt
4 teaspoons finely chopped lemon zest
2 tablespoons lemon juice

mighty mains

Lamb with Oranges and Anchovies	*107*
Braised Rabbit with Warm Lentil Salad	*108*
Salad of Roasted Vegetables in Yoghurt Pastry	*110*
Duck with Cardamom, Honey and Brandied Raisins	*111*
Apple Clafoutis with Peppered Raclette and Crisp Mint Salad	*112*
Venison with Ginger and Pasta Rosti	*114*
Horseradish-Crusted Beef with Winter Pesto and Vinegar-Baked Potatoes	*116*
Tajine of Chicken with Summer Tomato Jam	*118*
Buttered Noodles	*119*
Duck Pie with Port and Grapefruit	*120*
Beef with Mustard and Cognac	*122*
Crème Brûlée of Garlic with Smoked Salmon Croûtons	*124*
Monkfish with Lemon, Herbs and Vermouth	*126*
Shank of Lamb with Red Wine and Gherkins	*128*
Orange Tabbouleh	*129*
Fillet Steak with Old-Fashioned Stuffing, Green Peppercorns and Whisky	*130*
Pork with Rosemary and White Wine	*131*
Chicken with Plum and Walnuts	*132*
Chicken with Yoghurt and Red Pepper Coulis	*134*
Little Chickens in Sauternes	*136*

My parents taught us at an early age how to dine and converse at the same time, a feat that requires considerable social skills to avoid choking to death or spraying your siblings with mashed potato.

At dinner the main course always seems to be the most important stage. We have taken the edge off our hunger with soup and perhaps an entrée, we have dessert to look forward to, and we have a slow, gentle time in which to enjoy the most substantial course. Time to savour and appreciate food, and time to enjoy deep old-fashioned conversation.

In a family of six children the main evening meal was the most pleasant time of day. My father would amuse us, my mother would control the level of conversation and table manners, and my sister Virginia would invariably be told off as she giggled so much that no one would eat. We never touched our knife and fork until Father was seated, we would eat all that was put in front of us, and ask politely to leave the table when we had finished. For all that, we loved this time. We discussed school, friends, aspirations and problems at that table. We sang 'This old man', discussed holidays and trips to town, and talked about going fishing at Lake Coleridge. My father died when I was twelve, and my strongest memories of him are during this time when the whole family was together at the table.

In my view the main course is the most important. It is the course that provides health and balance, whether we have meat and three vegetables, a vegetarian gâteau with a salad of roasted vegetables, or lightly poached fish with mesclun salad. It is the main event, the moment when the clock slows, giving us time to catch our breath, to savour the stillness of the moment, and the bonding of family, friends and new acquaintances.

When planning a meal it is the occasion that directs the style and the main course that guides the menu. It is the colour, taste, balance and texture of the main course that will affect your choice of preceding and following courses.

In the restaurant menus must be planned with thought to both taste and, these days, the health of the customer. We are guided by the availability of ingredients, balance of sauces, textures, temperatures and so on. The catering chef is guided largely by the kitchen space available and the reason for the occasion. When designing a menu for a client it is vital to see the kitchen. There is nothing worse than arriving to find that the 'large family kitchen' is not only small, white and spotless, but it is a part of the family room where everyone is mingling for pre-dinner cocktails. Somehow you have to lay out food for 90, carry in buckets of cooked chicken, sort plastic bags of blanched vegetables, and heat bottles of sauces in water baths. As well you have to attempt to make

MIGHTY MAINS

all this look professional, polished and of course tidy.

In fact, when the menu is planned to suit the occasion and the facilities, everything is possible. We have catered for weddings of 120 out of small domestic kitchens, for theatre functions of 350 out of a bike shed, and very smart formal luncheons of 600 using the garden shed as the kitchen. I have served a full five-course silver-service meal for 40 on a private yacht with a kitchen the size of a small cupboard, and catered for 400 shareholders from a temporary kitchen put together in a carpark building.

One thing I have learnt, though, is that what works well in a restaurant, with its wonderful white-tiled stainless-steel kitchen and candlelit dining room, can be impossible to reproduce in a shearing shed, a marquee, or even a domestic kitchen. A restaurant menu is designed with an awareness of the equipment of the kitchen, the professionalism of the staff, and the staggered demands of the dining room. It is one thing to have four orders for beef cooked in a horseradish crust and serve it in the restaurant, but quite another at a function to serve 90 or even just 19 orders at once, and get them to the table all piping hot and perfectly cooked.

Menus for large numbers must include recipes that will hold well if the timetable is changed, will not curdle, overcook or be ruined should the power supply be erratic, and do not include offbeat ingredients that may offend guests' palates. If the menu is set, then a light meat for the main course is best; for example a breast of chicken with champagne and hazelnuts, with an entrée perhaps of salmon, and a dessert of triple chocolate flan with fresh strawberries. Choose a combination that will be acceptable to the majority, and follow the principle of 'less is best'.

It is wise to stick to Escoffier's famous dictum 'faites simple' in all menu planning. Whether it is a dinner party for 8 or for 80, it is hopeless to try to emulate a professional restaurant kitchen when you are working out of a domestic or a makeshift catering kitchen.

Professional cooking is full of tricks and short cuts. Cooking to order is an intensely pressurised business, and the old adage 'keep out of the kitchen if you can't stand the heat', referring to the pressure rather than the temperature, certainly holds true. No home cook or entertainer wants to have a menu that is so demanding they have to wear a sweat band and running shoes when they disappear into the depths of the kitchen.

Design the menu in a relaxed fashion. Pour yourself a glass of wine, sit down with your favourite collection of cookbooks or recipes and look at the occasion you wish to create. If you are the cook, the kitchenhand, host and waiter all wrapped up in one, then keep it simple. Have one difficult dish if you must, but design your menu so that if the drinks go on longer than anticipated it will not spoil the dinner. Remember too that the quality of a dish can never rise above that of its ingredients, so pick the freshest, best produce available.

Whatever happens with the food at a dinner party, or even a family dinner or impromptu meal for friends, enjoy it and never apologise if you make a mistake. It does not add to the enjoyment of an evening when the host or hostess makes comments like 'this would have been great if only I had not cooked the meat so much', or 'if only I hadn't added vinegar to the sauce'.

Your guests are there to enjoy the occasion and the company; so what if you forgot to salt the vegetables, overcooked the beef or boiled the asparagus to a shade of grey? You are not going for a guide rating. We all get things wrong sometimes and accidents happen; however, they are more likely to happen when we forget simplicity and approach a dinner with over-complicated recipes and unnecessarily fussy presentation.

This selection of main course recipes can be altered to suit your palate, or the occasion. Make them smaller for a luncheon, increase your favourite herb, or perhaps try a different meat with the sauce to suit the seasons. The vegetarian mains work beautifully as an entrée, and both the rabbit with olives and the chicken in yoghurt are heaven when cold.

> 'No home *cook* or *entertainer* wants to have *a menu* that is so demanding they have to wear *a sweat band* and running shoes when they *disappear into the depths of the kitchen*.'

Notes

If you have any juices left over from roasting lamb, or even chicken, use them to prepare a vinaigrette with substance. I substitute the juices for oil, or add a spoonful or two to oil and vinegar. The flavour is amazing, and has great depth. It's wonderful with a warm potato salad, excellent with tomatoes, and just perfect with a salad of rare lamb. Freeze the juices in ice-cube containers if you do not need them immediately — the size is just perfect.

Lamb *with* Oranges *and* Anchovies

This is the sort of dish I like to cook on Sunday when the restaurant is closed and family and friends gather for a relaxed meal at Governors Bay. My sister Andrea gave me this recipe some years ago. She lives on a yacht which she built herself, and has designed recipes that suit the small kitchen, yet give her the ability to entertain regularly. She's a good cook, with a love of Mediterranean flavours. This recipe is one of my favourites from her collection.

I must confess I have seen a leg of lamb cooked to this recipe fall out of its dish in a not-so-gentle sea, slide along the floor, stop at the wall of the bunk, slide back again and be scooped up, sliced and served with a smile. We loved it and lived to tell the tale.

Method

Preheat the oven to 200°C/400°F. Combine the olives, orange zest, sage, garlic, anchovies and pepper, and mix to a paste.

Lay the leg of lamb out on a board, skin side down and spread the inside of the lamb with the paste. Roll and tie at 5 cm (2 in) intervals with string that will stand the heat. If you like, make shallow incisions in the leg and insert a garlic sliver in each — you can never have too much of a good thing. Place the leg of lamb on a rack in a roasting pan, and for rare meat roast until a meat thermometer registers 120°C/250°F — I find it takes between 45 and 60 minutes. Cook it longer if you like your lamb well done or your oven is a little slow. Let the meat rest for 10 minutes before carving.

Slice the leg and serve it with mashed potatoes, French green beans, spinach or carrots. For a sauce I reserve about 3 tablespoons of the paste and whisk it with 1 cup of lamb stock. Serve this warm in a jug.

1 cup chopped olives, preferably nicoise or kalamata
zest of 1 orange
2 tablespoons freshly chopped sage
2 tablespoons minced garlic
2 tablespoons finely chopped anchovies
½ teaspoon freshly ground black pepper
1 leg of lamb, about 3 kg (6 lb), boned and butterflied
3 cloves garlic, slivered (optional)

Braised Rabbit *with* Warm Lentil Salad

1 fresh rabbit, jointed (see Notes)
2 cloves garlic, peeled and crushed
2 tablespoons finely chopped oregano
sea salt and freshly ground pepper
¼ cup red wine vinegar
¼ cup olive oil
1 cup small stoned prunes
½ cup stuffed olives, thinly sliced
¼ cup capers, plus 2 tablespoons of their liquid
2 bayleaves, crushed
¾ cup brown sugar
¾ cup white wine
2 tablespoons finely chopped parsley or coriander

Moist and tender, this is the most wonderfully elegant rabbit dish you're ever likely to encounter. Rabbit is a meat that is often overlooked, but as country children we were brought up on such delights as rabbit pie, jugged hare and daube of rabbit. My grandmother would cook rabbit in her large green coal range, slowly, gently, and the meat would be oh so moist.

In the restaurant we use the rabbit shoulder, as this cut is always meaty and tender. For the home cook a whole rabbit is more practical. This recipe is also good with chicken, quail or pheasant.

Method

In a large bowl combine the rabbit pieces, garlic, oregano, salt and pepper, vinegar, oil, prunes, olives, capers and liquid, and the bayleaves. Cover and allow to marinate for at least 4 hours but preferably overnight.

Heat the oven to 180°C/350°F. Arrange the rabbit in a shallow pan and spoon the marinade over it. Sprinkle with brown sugar and pour the wine around the rabbit. Bake for about 50 minutes, basting frequently. Transfer to a serving platter, moisten with the pan juices and sprinkle with the finely chopped herbs. Serve with the warm lentil salad and a sauceboat of the remaining juices from the rabbit. The juices may need to be thickened with slackened cornflour and seasoned.

Warm Lentil Salad

Roughly crush the black mustard seeds and half of the yellow seeds. Stir in the Dijon mustard, vinegar and 150 ml (¼ pt) of the olive oil. Add the spring onions and mix well. Season with sea salt and white pepper.

Bring a pot of salted water to the boil, add the lentils and simmer over medium heat for 15 minutes, until just tender. Drain and rinse well with boiling water. Tip the lentils into a bowl and pour the mustard dressing over them. Heat the remaining oil and mustard seeds together and cook until the mustard seeds pop. Tip in the lentils and warm through. Serve.

2 teaspoons black mustard seeds
2 teaspoons yellow mustard seeds
1 teaspoon Dijon mustard
1 tablespoon balsamic vinegar
180 mls olive oil
2 bunches spring onions, thinly sliced
8 tablespoons brown lentils, rinsed
sea salt and freshly ground white pepper

Resting meat

Resting meat is essential to achieve good flavour. When red meat cooks all the juices flow toward the centre. If you cut the meat too soon, the middle will be moist but the exterior dry. By allowing the meat to rest, the juices will permeate it evenly. We rest meat by sitting it on a plate, at an angle to drain any excess liquid away, and covered with another plate to keep it warm.

MIGHTY MAINS

Jointing a rabbit

First remove the liver, cover and refrigerate it. Trim off the flaps of skin, the tops of the forelegs and any excess bone. With a heavy knife or cleaver, divide the carcass crosswise into three sections — hind legs, saddle and forelegs. Cut between the hind legs to separate them into two pieces. Split the front carcass into two pieces in much the same way and split the saddle crosswise into three even pieces.

Thickening a sauce

If a sauce is too thin but has good flavour, do not hesitate to stabilise (lightly thicken) it with a slurry of cornflour. Dissolve the cornflour in a bit of cold stock or water, turn the sauce down to a simmer and stir the slurry into the sauce until it thickens. Do not bother to measure the cornflour, a tablespoon or so in water to make a slurry is all that is needed, and do not heat the sauce to boiling once the cornflour is added, or the starch will break down and leave a thin sauce again.

3 tablespoons light olive oil
1 cup peeled and coarsely chopped pumpkin
1 cup angle-sliced asparagus
1 cup mushrooms, sliced in half
1 cup coarsely chopped green beans
1 cup tomatoes, sliced into quarters
1 cup seeded and diced peppers
½ cup diced avocado
1 cup garlic cloves, skinned
8 spring onions, white part only
1 teaspoon cracked black pepper
½ teaspoon salt

125 g (4 oz) yoghurt
125 g (4 oz) butter at room temperature
300 g (9 oz) flour
¼ teaspoon salt

Salad *of* Roasted Vegetables *in* Yoghurt Pastry

This dish is very popular at Michaels. I acquired it from my first employers, Bert and Carol, two people who had a great effect on my early years in the restaurant world. More than twenty years later, they are still close friends, and whenever I am in doubt about any food matter I go back to my early training and ask myself what would they do . . . and all is well.

Method

Preheat the oven to 180°C/350°F.

Ensure the vegetable pieces are approximately the same size to allow for uniform cooking. Toss them in the olive oil and bake in the oven until well coloured. Season and chill before wrapping in yoghurt pastry.

Yoghurt *Pastry*

Combine all the ingredients in a large bowl and knead to a firm dough. Wrap the dough in plastic wrap and refrigerate for about 30 minutes.

Butter and flour 8 brioche tins. Roll the pastry out thinly and line the tins. Fill with the roasted vegetables and cut a circle of pastry for the top of each brioche tin. Refrigerate for another half-hour, then bake for about 25 minutes. Turn out and serve with a red pepper coulis (see page 135).

Notes

This recipe freezes well. When ready for use, put it in the oven straight from the freezer, and cook it a little longer (but don't burn it).

The recipe can be made up in a single loaf tin, as a free-form strudel roll on an oven tray, or as a gateâu in a 21 cm sponge tin.

Add some grated cheese to strengthen flavour, some fresh herbs, wine-soaked currants or even cumin. Alter the flavours to suit the vegetables you have available. Basil would be perfect with summer vegetables, marjoram with autumn fare and perhaps some rosemary with heavier winter produce.

If including asparagus in your vegetable selection, add orange zest and finely chopped mint; add nutmeg with kumara.

Duck *with* Cardamom, Honey *and* Brandied Raisins

I remember preparing this dish one weekend at Denbrae, my sister Geraldine's farm. I worked as sous-chef, and we went about preparing several dishes for the evening's meal. The occasion was a thank-you to locals who had managed to put out a fire in the haybarn a few weeks before, and we were expecting twelve for dinner. Although there is quite a list of ingredients, this is a very simple recipe; throw it together, slide it into the oven and forget it. The brandied raisins we had in the pantry, but I include a simple recipe that is very successful. I always make these raisins up in winter as the smell is so pleasant in the house!

The honey was local and strong, but we have also made this recipe with mild table honey and it is just as good.

2 ducks, cut into quarters and browned
3 large onions, finely chopped
2 bayleaves
1 tablespoon fresh thyme
2 cloves garlic, finely chopped
1 tablespoon each cardamom, ginger, allspice and cinnamon
zest of 1 orange
1½ tablespoons honey
1 teaspoon salt and pinch of black pepper
1 cup each red wine, orange juice and water

Method

Preheat the oven to 180°C/350°F.

Combine all the ingredients and pour them over the duck. Braise in the oven in a covered dish until cooked and ready to serve; it takes 1½ hours in the Aga on the farm, and just over 2 hours in my oven at Governors Bay. I prefer to cook a dish with this mixture of flavours slowly and gently so all the flavours mingle. Once cooked, check the seasoning again. The sauce may need to be reduced to give a coating consistency, and any 'eyes' of fat that may be floating on the sauce should be removed with kitchen towels.

Serve accompanied by brandied raisins, orange zest and a little cracked pepper sprinkled on the plate.

Brandied Raisins

Heat the raisins in the water. Drain, reserving the liquid, and add the brandy to the raisins. Place in 2 screwtop jars. Heat the liquid from the raisins with the honey and reduce to about 1 cup of liquid in total. Pour gently over the raisins and seal. Store in the refrigerator or a cool larder.

750 g (1½ lb) raisins
1.2 l (2 pints) water
¾ cup brandy
¼ cup liquid honey

Notes

To divide a duck into quarters, use a sharp knife and cut the bird in half lengthways and then in half again. Slide the knife under the leg and cut straight down for best effect.

After grilling a steak I often deglaze the pan with a splash of port, a little beef stock and a generous tablespoon of these brandied raisins. Simmer for a moment, add a knob of butter to the sauce, off the heat, and whisk. Pour the sauce over the thickly sliced steak. Very French, with a hint of American sweetness.

Brandied raisins are also excellent with such desserts as cappuccino ice cream, rich dark chocolate and coffee cakes, and ginger ices. Also wonderful with cheese.

Apple Clafoutis *with* Peppered Raclette *and* Crisp Mint Salad

A main course without meat can be exciting, and this dish is no exception. The clafoutis can be served in classical fashion at a formal dinner party; in terracotta pots, rustic style, for lunch; or for Sunday tea on that blue and white dinner set you got as a wedding present years ago. It's a great dish, and just because it has no dead animal component does not mean it is not illustrious enough to be a main course.

I have often referred, without malice, to vegetarians as the 'brown rice brigade', walking around in flowing clothing, looking very serious about the state of their aura, and deeply concerned about the greenhouse effect and the alignment of the stars. Naive to say the least. My mother's mother, who was born in Dublin in 1894, was with a few exceptions a vegetarian, and not only did she play the violin and collect excellent art and antiques but she died at 98, cultured, well-read and a class act to boot. Perhaps she saw what I am only now beginning to see — that vegetarian food can taste great and be good for you, and that we do not have to follow the flock and have meat and three vegetables all the time. If we had to kill what we ate, just how many of us would still be meat-eaters?

This recipe is an example of how the total effect of a dish depends not on its individual components, but rather on how they are combined. Apples, raclette, cream and mint — an unusual combination, but heavenly. The use of cream in this dish may be a concern to some, but when you want to make a special dish quickly, without the benefit of stock, there is no better ingredient than cream to add volume, body and that velvety mouth feel. A clafoutis without cream is like an aeroplane without wings. Even nutritionists agree that occasional small amounts of butter and cream have their place. To indulge all the time is another matter.

Mint Salad

Combine the olive oil, lemon juice, mustard and sugar. Whisk until emulsified. Toss a small amount through the mint leaves until they are lightly coated. Put to one side.

1 tablespoon virgin olive oil
1 teaspoon fresh lemon juice
1 teaspoon Dijon mustard
½ cup sugar
2 cups fresh whole leaf mint

Clafoutis

60 g (2 oz) butter
3 apples, peeled, cored and sliced
2 tablespoons flour
3 eggs
5 tablespoons cream
200 g (6 oz) raclette
salt and freshly ground pepper

Preheat the oven to 180°C/350°F.

Melt the butter in a heavy sauté pan and fry the apples briefly until they begin to brown. Sprinkle with the flour and cook, stirring, for 2 minutes. Meanwhile mix the eggs and cream in a bowl, seasoning well. Stir in the apples and divide the mixture between four 10 cm (4 in) buttered tartlet tins. Bake for 15 minutes or until set and lightly coloured. In the last 2 minutes of cooking, slice the raclette into 4 wedges and toss these wedges in ground pepper. Sit a wedge on top of each clafoutis and warm until the raclette is just beginning to melt.

Remove from the oven and place each on a plate with the mint salad piled to one side. Serve with crunchy French bread and a glass of excellent Merlot.

Peppercorns

As a seasoning whole white or black peppercorns, ground at the last moment from a peppermill, add unparalleled flavour and give a dish a 'finish'. Pre-ground pepper can quickly become stale, adding a harsh, acrid flavour to food. Sometimes, however, as in this dish, large amounts of freshly ground coarse pepper are needed. In my kitchens I grind whole peppercorns in a small electric coffee grinder to get a large amount of freshly ground coarse pepper. At home I use a heavy meat cleaver to crush the peppercorns.

Venison *with* Ginger *and* Pasta Rosti

One year when I was in San Francisco I had the good fortune to work alongside Dewayne Lumpkin, an innovative and very talented art dealer who loved to cook, loved to eat, but above all loved art. Dewayne introduced me to pasta sautéed as a rosti, and at a dinner party we played around with the flavour which I felt would go well with our New Zealand farmed venison. After a few wicked disasters we came up with this recipe, which has been served with pride to friends not only in San Francisco, Sydney and Auckland, but Paris and Melbourne as well.

I enjoy the flavour of ginger, tomato and garlic combined, making an almost Portuguese-flavoured sauce. Although this recipe is slightly more complicated than your basic sautéed venison fillet, the extra steps pay off in flavour and taste sophistication. Cooking the sauce separately and reducing it makes a more complex, flavoursome sauce, and the added step of passing the sauce through a sieve and then adding the ginger and tomato results in a more elegant presentation. For all its flavours, when well cooked this dish is mild but far from bland. It's even better if it is prepared a day in advance, allowing the flavours to mellow.

In fact, this is one dish where you can make up the sauce well in advance, make up the pasta rosti three days in advance, and sauté the venison at the eleventh hour. It is a wonderful dish for the last-minute entertainer, for both the sauce and the rosti hold beautifully in the freezer in airtight containers for up to a month, leaving only the meat to deal with at the last minute.

125 g (4 oz) butter
2 tablespoons finely diced shallots or young onions
2 tablespoons finely diced fresh ginger
2 cloves garlic, mashed with a pinch of salt
1 teaspoon ground ginger
⅓ cup flour
3 cups good venison or beef stock
½ cup white wine
1 tablespoon tomato paste
2 tablespoons brown sugar
1 tablespoon lemon juice
2 tablespoons sherry vinegar
generous amount of black pepper
½ cup julienned crystallised ginger
½ cup skinned, seeded and diced tomatoes

Ginger Sauce

Combine the first 5 ingredients and cook until the shallots are lightly coloured. Add the flour and brown well. Add all the remaining ingredients except the crystallised ginger and the diced tomato. Simmer gently and reduce the liquid by one-third. Pass the sauce through a fine sieve and put it into a clean pot. Heat it gently, check the seasonings and add the ginger and tomato. Heat for 5 minutes for the flavours to mingle, and serve with the sautéed venison.

Pasta *Rosti*

Toss the noodles with the walnut oil, chopped walnuts, salt, chives and onion. Heat a small non-stick pan over high heat and add enough of the grapeseed oil to glaze

MIGHTY MAINS

the pan. When the pan is hot enough to sizzle add a handful of the noodles, patting them out into an even layer about 2 cm (¾ in) deep.

Cook until the noodles are golden on the bottom, adjusting the heat so they sizzle without scorching — this takes about 8 minutes. Turn and cook the other side. Drizzle a bit more oil down the side of the pan if it looks too dry. Drain the rosti on paper towels and keep warm in the oven. Repeat with the remaining noodles. Alternatively the rosti can be cooked in a large pan and cut into wedges.

If the rosti have been frozen, reheat in a 170°C/325°F oven just before serving. They hold well but may need a drizzle of oil to keep up the moisture. The ideal is a rosti that is crisp on the outside, and moist and walnut flavoured on the inside. A perfect marriage with the venison.

250 g (8 oz) Chinese egg noodles, cooked, refreshed and drained
2 teaspoons walnut oil
2 tablespoons finely chopped walnuts
1 teaspoon salt
2 tablespoons finely chopped chives
2 tablespoons finely chopped onion
5 tablespoons grapeseed or olive oil

Venison

Trim the venison of all its blue skin and sinew. Cut slices 1 cm thick and toss quickly in the salt, pepper and marjoram. Heat the butter and oil together in a solid sauté pan over high heat and sauté the venison quickly to seal and barely cook it. Venison of this calibre should always be cooked rare, or medium-rare at the most, but no more, as there is no fat in the meat to keep it moist. Toss the venison through the ginger sauce, pile up onto the pasta rosti and drizzle the whole dish with more sauce; serve extra sauce to one side and dust the entire dish with a light sprinkling of paprika.

2 midloins of venison
½ teaspoon sea salt
½ teaspoon freshly ground black pepper
1 teaspoon finely chopped marjoram
30 g (1 oz) butter
2 tablespoons oil
paprika for garnish

Horseradish-Crusted Beef *with* Winter Pesto *and* Vinegar-Baked Potatoes

It is amazing how a recipe brings back memories of childhood. This family recipe comes from my father's twin sisters, our favourite aunts, who would listen to all the dreams of our youth, the agonies of adolescence, and the drama of adulthood. They would sit in their sitting room surrounded by a dozen cats, all the family silver, and the horse trots blaring on the radio. Their garden was immaculate, the freezers full of beans, and the drinks cabinet always held the welcoming whisky. And boy, could they cook a dinner to feed an army! This was one of the recipes we all looked forward to — is there anything better than a golden, moist fillet of beef?

This is the most simple of dishes. A little forethought, some pre-planning, and on the evening it will take two minutes' work. The idea of potatoes cooked with vinegar is innovative and the flavour is glorious. I have served this dish as a main course at formal dinners, at simple family celebrations, and cold at corporate picnics.

The meat is wonderful hot, with the pesto to one side and accompanied by the potatoes. It's great warm as a luncheon dish or relaxed family dinner, and believe it or not it is just superb cold at a picnic, with the pesto to complete and lift the flavour and the potato served exactly as is, salad style at room temperature.

My Aunt Joan would cook this as a whole fillet, wrap it in tinfoil and pack it up to take to the Rakaia Gorge with a tomato and red onion salad made with malt vinegar dressing, a creamy slaw and the vinegar potatoes. We would set off early with our fishing rods and tackle, our bait and numerous chocolate bars, and follow her to the favourite family spot. I loathe fishing — it seems to take forever to catch what I could buy in five minutes — but I loved the food, and sure as eggs I'd be there looking enthusiastic, waiting for lunch.

Horseradish-*Crusted* Beef

Combine the flour, salt, pepper and horseradish in a shallow tray; the eggs, salt, horseradish and garlic in another; and the salt, pepper, onion, parsley and

4 fillet steaks, 150 g (5 oz) each, or 1 whole fillet
oil or butter
½ cup flour
½ teaspoon each sea salt and freshly ground black pepper
½ teaspoon finely grated fresh horseradish (optional)
2 eggs, lightly beaten
¼ teaspoon salt
2 teaspoons horseradish, fresh or paste
2 cloves garlic, mashed
½ teaspoon each sea salt and freshly ground black pepper
1 small onion, finely chopped
4 tablespoons finely chopped parsley
1 cup dried breadcrumbs

◆ MIGHTY MAINS

2 cups loosely packed parsley
1 tablespoon finely chopped thyme
1 teaspoon finely chopped rosemary
2 tablespoons grated parmesan
1 tablespoon coarsely chopped walnuts
2 cloves garlic, peeled and coarsely chopped
½ cup olive oil
salt and pepper to taste

breadcrumbs in another. Sauté the fillets on a very hot grill for about 2 minutes on each side. Put to one side and chill. Toss the beef, whole or in steaks, in the seasoned flour, the egg mixture and finally the crumbs. Chill well.

Drizzle the steaks with a little butter and bake in the oven at 200°C/400°F until well coloured and cooked to the desired degree, or heat about 4 cm of grapeseed oil in a frying pan until very hot and cook the steaks until crisp. It is very important to have the oil very hot or it will be absorbed by the crust and be most unpleasant.

Serve crisp and hot, with the winter pesto and potatoes to accompany, or let it cool and pack for later use.

Winter *Pesto*

Place the herbs, parmesan, walnuts and garlic in a processor. While the machine is running, slowly drizzle in the olive oil. More may be needed if you prefer a lighter pesto. Season to taste and store until needed.

Potatoes in Vinegar

Preheat the oven to 170°C/325°F. Peel the onions and put them to one side. Peel away a 0.5 cm (¼ in) thick band of skin from around each potato. Place the onions and potatoes in a baking dish just large enough to hold them. Melt the butter and pour it, and the vinegar, over the potatoes and onions. Add the salt and pepper and mix until they are coated. Bury the thyme sprigs in the vegetables and cover the dish with foil. Bake in the oven for 2 hours, stirring the vegetables each half-hour to recoat them. Be sure to cover them after stirring. When cooked, the onions and potatoes will be a deep brown colour.

12 small white onions, about the size of golf balls
12 red potatoes, also about the size of golf balls
60 g (2 oz) butter
3 tablespoons balsamic vinegar
½ teaspoon salt
freshly ground black pepper
6 sprigs thyme

Notes

Although they are good with just about any roasted or grilled meat and poultry, I like to serve these potatoes and onions with braised dishes. The potatoes are peeled only around the middle, giving the look of a cummerbund. This not only gives them an appealing look, but allows the vinegar to penetrate during the slow roast. To give a good even roast, turn the vegetables about every 30 minutes.

Pepper

There seems to be a great debate among cooks about the superiority of black pepper over white. Many chefs prefer the more aromatic, assertive flavour of the unripe dried peppercorn, or black peppercorn, to that of the white peppercorn, produced from ripe berries that have been washed of their outer layer and then sun-dried. White peppercorns are slightly milder, and in general I much prefer using freshly ground white pepper both for its subtle flavour and for its appearance. On the other hand, black pepper is great in recipes such as this, with steaks, mussels, well-flavoured smoked foods and most red meats.

Tajine *of* Chicken *with* Summer Tomato Jam

In my early days of entertaining, I can recall one occasion where I really wanted to impress my guests and spent hours in the kitchen. Unfortunately I was so anxious I panicked over the outcome and basically created a disaster by getting stressed. Not good. Now I always remind students that when you entertain at home you should not let the food be in control. Your friends aren't coming to see a chicken, they are coming to see you.

With this recipe, however, I am not so sure. An adaptation of a Moroccan recipe, the combination of honey, cinnamon and chilli with tomato, plus the gentle flavour of chicken, is a blow-out. The jam can be made separately and well in advance. It's a great pantry item — just make it up and freeze it until you decide to entertain. Pour the mixture over the chicken and braise gently.

Because of its simplicity and ease of preparation this is an invaluable recipe. It is one that has been used numerous times, not only in the restaurant but at dinner parties around the world, for it has become a favourite at the school for students who wish to learn the art of entertaining with ease, and of course with style as well. It is excellent served on the pasta rosti from the venison with ginger and pasta rosti (page 114), with nut rice or even buttered noodles (see opposite).

Chicken *Tajine*

Put the chicken in a shallow dish, mix the remaining seasoning ingredients to a paste and rub into the flesh of the chicken. Put aside to marinate while preparing the jam.

Once the jam has thickened to a coating consistency, pour it over the chicken. Place in a moderate oven (180°C/350°F) for about 30 minutes; the juices should run clear when the chicken is pricked with a skewer.

1 chicken, cut into quarters
4 cloves garlic, skinned
½ teaspoon sea salt
¼ teaspoon turmeric
¼ teaspoon ground ginger
freshly ground white pepper

Summer Tomato Jam

2 tablespoons oil
1 onion, finely chopped
1 tablespoon turmeric
1 tablespoon ground ginger
2 tablespoons cinnamon
6 cloves garlic, crushed
1.5 kg (3 lb) good ripe tomatoes, skins removed
4 tablespoons honey
cayenne, freshly ground white pepper and salt to taste
tomato paste (optional)

Place the onion, turmeric, ginger and cinnamon in a pot with the oil and cook for 5 minutes. Add all the remaining ingredients and slowly bring to a simmer; reduce for about 30 minutes and check seasoning.

The tomato paste will only be needed if the tomatoes do not have good colour or flavour. The amount of cayenne, salt and pepper is entirely personal. I like a lot of heat and add freshly ground red chilli as well.

Once the jam has thickened to a coating consistency, pour it over the marinated chicken. Place in a moderate oven (180°C/350°F) for about 30 minutes; the juices should run clear when the chicken is pricked with a skewer.

Notes

Tinned tomatoes are excellent for this dish. The Italian plum tomatoes seem to give the best results.

The jam can be bottled and sealed for much later use; we have kept our jam base for up to six months this way, but it may keep longer.

Buttered Noodles

250 g (8 oz) fresh egg noodles, cooked and chilled
3 tablespoons good chicken stock
2 tablespoons clarified butter
3 tablespoons diced crystallised ginger
3 tablespoons coarsely chopped toasted brazil nuts
zest of 2 lemons
3 tablespoons roasted sesame seeds

Heat a non-stick frypan and add the stock and butter, toss in the noodles to quickly heat and add all the remaining ingredients. Season.

These noodles are as versatile as the chicken. They can be stored in the fridge, reheat perfectly, and are heaven-sent to a busy family cook. Excellent with the addition of the coarsely chopped brazil nuts, or almonds.

Duck Pie *with* Port *and* Grapefruit

I believe it's important not to be afraid to try new ingredients, to feel free to make risky combinations. How else can we reach the sublime? And if an experiment fails you can always order a pizza.

This delightful recipe developed when we were playing around with flavours at the Small Kitchen School. We came up with a combination that has not only been taught at the school but has been served at many a function. Made smaller, this is an excellent combination of flavours for a first course. Bake it as a large pastry tart to slice and serve at a buffet or eat it cold as part of a tailgate picnic.

The recipe looks complicated but in reality it has three simple stages that can be prepared well in advance. It is perfect for a formal dinner. It freezes well, but do cook it straight from the freezer, at a lower temperature and for longer than usual. I prefer to cook pastry at a lower temperature than most recipes state, as I find the layers get cooked to a lovely nut brown. Perhaps this is just being a fussy cook.

1 duck, about 2.5 kg (5 lb)
2 tablespoons olive oil
90 g (3 oz) finely diced onion
125 g (4 oz) finely diced carrot
½ cup stock
½ cup port
zest and juice of 1 orange
1 tablespoon brown sugar
1 clove garlic

Method

Wash the duck and pat it dry. Heat the olive oil in a large saucepan and gently brown the duck. Add the onion and carrot, and continue to sauté. Add all the remaining ingredients and simmer for 1–1½ hours until the duck is cooked. Take the bird out of the stock, cool and remove all the meat, shred it and put it in the fridge.

The skin, bones and fat from the duck should be returned to the stock, simmered for 20 minutes to release the maximum amount of flavour, then strained again. Chill the stock to set the fat. Use this stock in the sauce and freeze any that is left for later use. Freeze the fat as well for sauté cooking.

125 g (4 oz) diced smoked bacon
200 g (6 oz) sliced button mushrooms
125 g (4 oz) toasted flaked almonds
½ cup finely chopped parsley
1 grapefruit, skinned and segmented

Pie Filling

Sauté the bacon and mushrooms and combine with all the other ingredients, plus the shredded duck meat.

Grapefruit *Sauce*

To make the sauce, heat the butter and add the flour. Cook until well coloured as this will give the sauce a good nutty flavour. Bring the stock to the boil and gradually add this to the flour and butter mixture, stirring constantly. Reduce to a simmer, add the cream and grapefruit juice and season. Simmer to reduce slightly, about 20 minutes.

125 g (4 oz) butter
90 g (3 oz) flour
1.25 litres (2 pints) duck or chicken stock
200 ml (8 fl oz) cream
juice of 1 grapefruit

To *Create* Individual Pies

Puff pastry
1 egg and a pinch of salt

Preheat oven to 180°C/350°F.

Roll the pastry out thinly and cut it into 10 cm (4 in) squares. Place about 2 tablespoons of the duck mixture on each piece of pastry, brush the edges with the egg/salt glaze, and draw the pastry up at the corners to form a small triangle-shaped pie. Brush the pies with the egg and chill well. Bake until golden, about 20 minutes.

Serve the pies on a small pool of the sauce, with honeyed wholegrain mustard, perhaps a couscous pilaf and a side salad with crisp fried bacon and for sharpness some segments of grapefruit.

I also love this with glazed turnip as a vegetable. To glaze turnip, simply peel and cut the turnips into 1 cm (½ in) dice, toss through a little melted butter, a few drops of sesame oil and a sprinkling of chicken stock, roast in the oven until cooked and lightly glazed. More stock may be needed but the turnip will give up a lot of water as it is roasted.

Beef *with* Mustard *and* Cognac

This is another great dish for entertaining, for all the work is done ahead of time. It is a rich, delicious main course that cries out for creamy mashed potatoes, sautéed asparagus and a glass of tannic red wine — elegant, yet homely, and irresistible. Make the sauce separately, the day before if it makes for an easier life.

When serving fillet steak, the focus is on the sauce and occasionally the accompaniments. Flavours need to be strong to stand up to the meat. The great thing about steak is that it can be handled quickly and in a straightforward manner. It's a fast jump from pan to plate, so if you treat each cut of steak properly, you will have the satisfaction of providing a delicious meal with no fuss.

I like to marinate my steak in a little oil and cracked pepper overnight, and in the restaurant when we cut our steaks we always lay them in good oil, to assist with the aging and make them simple to grill; it does give a much better product. Do not add salt at this stage as it will draw out the blood and give you a dry fillet.

When dealing with steak your most important friend is your butcher. Stick to a good butchery, have them explain how they cut the meat, let them know if your steak was good, and inform them if you were disappointed. If you are going to indulge in meat, let it be the best available.

Fillet steak should always be served rare or medium-rare — never well done, which toughens the meat. And do not rush to serve meat when it has finished cooking, it needs to relax to distribute the juices evenly. Since fillet is naturally tender it does not need a long cooking time. Doneness is not a guessing game, or a matter of 'cut it up and see what it looks like inside'. You can recognise when meat is done to your liking, by touch. The best trick was shown to me when I was having classes at a small French restaurant in Los Angeles. The chef pointed out that if you like meat rare, it feels somewhat like the muscle between the thumb and index finger when it is relaxed. When you stretch your fingers, the muscle tightens, resembling medium-cooked meat. When meat feels like the muscle in a clenched fist, it has had its day, unless you like your meat very well done.

Method

Sauté the shallots in butter until lightly coloured. Add half the Cognac and flambé. Add the flour and cook. Add the stock, lemon juice, mustards, salt, pepper and turmeric and simmer for 10 minutes. Add the cream and remaining Cognac. Strain the sauce and hold in a bain-marie until needed. This sauce will also hold in a thermos until the steaks are cooked.

Grill steaks to the desired degree and place each in the middle of a large dinner

60 g (2 oz) finely chopped shallots
60 g (2 oz) butter
½ cup Cognac
60 g (2 oz) flour
2 cups good brown stock
1 tablespoon lemon juice
1 tablespoon Dijon mustard
1 teaspoon dry mustard
½ teaspoon sea salt
½ teaspoon ground white pepper
½ teaspoon turmeric
1 cup cream
6 fillet steaks

MIGHTY MAINS

plate. Pour 2 tablespoons of sauce over and around, and serve extra sauce in a jug. If you wish, a light dusting of finely chopped skinned and seeded tomato or fresh herbs would add a little colour to the steak, or add a simple sprig of fresh thyme or chervil.

Remember that we eat with our eyes first, but also remember not to over-garnish, and make sure the garnish marries in with the flavours of the dish. I am not a great believer in fruit, flowers or smart cut vegetables, which are often time-consuming and not well thought out.

Salt

Salt is essential to good cooking and really should not be considered an optional seasoning. Salt brings to life the flavours of an ingredient, adding body to a dish, balancing the flavour in pastry and giving finish to sauces and soups.

Over the years I have partaken in various salt tastings and found the experience invaluable. I have tried the same dish salted with sea salt, rock salt, Maldon, kosher and common salt, and the difference in the effect is fascinating. Sea salt is my favourite. It is extracted from sea water by evaporation, while common rock salt is found in its crystalline state in the ground. I prefer Maldon salt for dishes where the magical, flaky salt is spread quickly and absorbed without any heating, and I loathe the metallic, almost chemical, flavour of common table and kosher salt.

Crème Brûlée *of* Garlic *with* Smoked Salmon Croûtons

In the mid-eighties, after I had had Michael's Restaurant for several years, I began to attend cooking classes in Auckland. By very good luck I met Lauraine Jacobs, a relaxed, knowledgeable and very generous foodie. Lauraine understood my hunger for knowledge, my warped sense of humour and my desire to get to know other areas of the food world. With her own zany style of humour, her professional attitude and her strong belief in New Zealand food, she was able to guide me through some difficult patches. A tower of knowledge, Lauraine is one of the people who has influenced me most in New Zealand. She never objected to being phoned at unusual hours to explain a technique, help with a food combination or advise me about writing, promotion or demonstration techniques. To know your job well is great, but to be unfailingly generous with your knowledge to an enthusiastic and somewhat naive foodie is something quite different.

During one of our many discussions over a glass of wine we talked about vegetable custards — whether they gave a good flavour to a dish, had too much cream, were too rich for summer, too light for winter, etc. I began to think about using garlic, and on the flight back to Christchurch I created in my head this dish for a crème brûlée of garlic. That night I cooked it, and the following week I used it at a sophisticated finger-food party, accompanied by these little smoked salmon croûtons. It was a great success. I have used it since as a first course, served in small individual ramekins with generous slabs of hot-smoked salmon and lightly poached fresh asparagus. It is a simple dish that lends itself to many variations — another dish with which to let your imagination flow, your hands wander in the pantry, and your talent soar.

Crème Brûlée *of Garlic*

Preheat the oven to 150°C/300°F.

Place the garlic in a small saucepan with water to cover and bring to the boil. Drain and repeat the process twice more, keeping the water for making stock later.

1 cup peeled garlic cloves
1 cup milk
1 cup cream
7 egg yolks
1 teaspoon salt
freshly ground black pepper to taste
½ cup freshly grated parmesan

MIGHTY MAINS

Place the milk, cream, yolks and blanched garlic in a blender and purée until the mixture is smooth. Season with salt and pepper and pass through a fine sieve. Pour into an ovenproof dish and place this in a large roasting pan. Pour hot water around so the dish is contained in a bain-marie, or water bath.

Bake the brûlée until the custard is set and a knife inserted into the centre comes out clean, about an hour. While this is cooking make the smoked salmon croûtons.

Remove the brûlée from the bain-marie, sprinkle with parmesan and either sit under a preheated grill until golden brown or brush with a blow-torch. Leave the brûlée in its dish and serve the warm salmon croûtons to one side. Have a spatula for guests to help themselves.

Smoked *Salmon* Croûtons

1 French bread stick
90 g (3 oz) butter
60 g (2 oz) smoked salmon
zest of 1 lemon
¼ teaspoon cracked white pepper

Slice the French bread thinly and dry it out in the oven. Combine the butter, smoked salmon, lemon zest and white pepper in a kitchen whizz. Spread this on the bread and bake in the oven until golden.

Notes

The brûlée can be made well in advance and gently reheated just before guests arrive.

We serve this brûlée with just about anything that goes with garlic and complements the rest of the food to be served. It's great with such accompaniments as a selection of crudités, crisp breadsticks wrapped in bacon, tiny pumpkin and herb scones served warm wrapped in linen napkins, plain warm toast, peppered waffles and, a favourite of mine, cayenne shortbread.

The smoked salmon croûtons can be replaced with croûtons made with other compound butters. An olive butter is a classic combination which complements the garlic perfectly, fresh herb butter enriched with lemon and black pepper is another, or butter combined with roasted pumpkin and finely chopped walnuts.

Monkfish *with* Lemon, Herbs *and* Vermouth

Of all the food that I have cooked, enjoyed and served, this is one of my favourites. It is very simple, for it is not always necessary to create a masquerade around fish. I have a friend who refers to overworked fish as looking like an old lady with too much make-up.

Chefs love to prepare fish because we can create recipes with light stocks, something we cannot do with meat. Low in fat, it has much to offer the health-conscious and there are few other products that are as fast and easy to prepare.

In my cooking I have a passion for both lusty peasant dishes and elegant modern offerings. This dish is a little of both. It comes from the very heart of my being. The basic idea of the sauce is from my close friend, fellow cook and food addict Sophia Magdalene. We have lightened the flavours, increased the herbs and brought in the vegetables for crunch.

Monkfish, often called 'poor man's crayfish', is a moist, tender and almost lush fish to work with; it is my preference every time. Combined with the lemon and vermouth, it is just magic.

With recipes increasingly being simplified and pared down to their hearts, like artichokes, each component must have maximum flavour for the dish to be successful. This one is a perfect example — the soft flavour of the monkfish, the lift of the fresh herbs, the crunch of the spring vegetables, and the kick of the vermouth.

Lemon Vermouth Sauce

60 g (2 oz) finely chopped onion
2 cm (1 in) ginger, finely chopped
4 cloves garlic, crushed
30 g (1 oz) butter
½ cup vermouth
1 cup fish stock
zest and juice of 1 lemon
2 tablespoons finely chopped herbs (e.g. parsley, chives, fennel, tarragon)
sea salt and tabasco to season
cream (optional)

Make the sauce before cooking the fish.

Sauté the onion, ginger and garlic in butter until soft and translucent. Add the vermouth and stock and simmer for 10 minutes to allow the flavours to marry. Pass the sauce through a fine sieve, pressing it well to extract the juices. Slacken a little cornflour in water and thicken the sauce. Heat but do not boil it. Strain the sauce again and add the lemon juice, fresh herbs and a little cream if you wish. (Retain the lemon zest for garnishing.) Check seasonings.

MIGHTY MAINS

Poached *Monkfish*

In a pan heat the 2 cups stock and gently lay the fish fillets in it. Do not boil, but heat until the fish is firm and has whitened in colour. Hold to one side in the stock.

Blanch the matchsticks of finely sliced vegetables in a pot of boiling water for about 30 seconds, drop instantly into ice-chilled water to set the colour and drain on paper towels. I often dry the vegetables in a lettuce spinner, which does a grand job.

To serve, sit the julienned vegetables on top of the poached fish and let them heat through for the last 2 minutes of cooking. Lift the fish and the vegetables out of the stock with a slotted spoon, and place in the middle of a large plate. Pour over about 2 tablespoons of sauce and dust with lemon zest and cracked pepper. Serve immediately.

I like to serve this dish with new potatoes, if they are in season, and a green salad. It has such a refreshing flavour that you do not want too many additions to mask the effect. Just stand back and be proud, and if your arms are long enough, pat yourself on the back.

2 cups good fish stock
6 medium-sized fillets monkfish
200 g (6 oz) julienred spring vegetables (carrots, snowpeas, young celery, asparagus, peppers)
cracked pepper

Shank *of* Lamb *with* Red Wine *and* Gherkins

If this dish is any indication, meals made from leftovers can be every bit as good as those that are laboured over in classical cuisine. People complain that they do not have time to slow-cook a dish like this, but time cannot buy what this dish offers in terms of outright satisfaction.

I have always enjoyed a good shank of lamb, the meat glutinous and flavoursome. It is the part of the leg that every child in a large family has fought over. Originally we thought of creating a red wine bisque and adding the shredded meat from the shank to make a dish that would be perfect for a winter's night. We discussed, cooked and discussed again, and decided this was the best recipe. We used some red wine that no one wanted and was still good quality, a jar of gherkins that had not sealed in our fit of bottling the week before, and some ham off the bone that we did not really want to freeze as it goes too watery. The addition of the juice from the bottled gherkins is the ultimate in using up leftovers, and it also gives the sauce a good bite. And the leftovers from this recipe could easily be turned into a soup for the kitchen staff with the addition of some stock.

I like to serve the shank in a large pasta bowl, sitting on a mound of couscous or tabbouleh, with the sauce poured all around. Serve it with bread, a green salad, creamy mashed potatoes and a crisp hot broccoli salad. Whichever way you serve it you will find the effect of the red wine and gherkins on the moist, tender meat is just perfect.

60 g (2 oz) butter
1 teaspoon paprika
4 large onions, finely chopped
60 g (2 oz) flour
8 cups good beef or lamb stock
2 cups red wine, sugared if wine is a little bitter
4 cloves garlic, crushed
1 tablespoon lemon juice
½ cup yoghurt
1 cup finely diced ham
1 cup finely diced gherkins
sea salt and freshly ground black pepper
juice from the gherkins, to taste
6 lamb shanks

Method

Sweat the onions in the butter with the paprika. Add the

MIGHTY MAINS

flour and cook the roux until coloured. Add the stock, wine, crushed garlic, lemon juice and yoghurt. Bring to a simmer and add the ham and gherkins. Check the seasoning as it may need sugar, salt and pepper and a little of the juice from the gherkins. The sauce should be well flavoured and have a very light coating texture.

Trim the shanks of any excess fat. Place them in a roasting dish and pour the sauce over them. Cover with foil and cook at 160°C/325°F for 2 hours. Check every half-hour that there is enough liquid and add more stock if necessary. The shanks are cooked when all the meat is tender and just beginning to come away from the bone.

These shanks reheat well, and freeze in their sauce perfectly. They can be shredded and tossed with a little vinaigrette combined with the sauce, and turned into an exquisite plated salad.

Orange *Tabbouleh*

This is wonderful with the shank. It also stores well and is great at Christmas with turkey.

Method

Generously cover the burghul wheat with hot water and let it stand for 30 minutes. Drain well and squeeze out all the water. Combine all the other ingredients and toss through the wheat. Check the seasoning and serve. If the tabbouleh is lacking in flavour, increase the amount of French dressing.

200 g (6 oz) burghul wheat
8 tablespoons finely chopped parsley
2 oranges, rind grated and segments finely chopped
1 small red pepper, finely chopped
3 tablespoons olive oil
4 tablespoons lemon juice
½ teaspoon cinnamon
½ teaspoon ground coriander
salt and freshly ground white pepper
¼ cup French dressing (see Basics)
2 tablespoons finely diced spring onion

Fillet Steak *with* Old-Fashioned Stuffing, Green Peppercorns *and* Whisky

2 medium onions, peeled and finely chopped
2 cloves garlic, minced
200 g (6 oz) butter
4 cups bread cubes, cut about 0.5 cm (¼ in) from plain white bread or brioche
2 tablespoons finely chopped fine herbs (parsley, chives, dill, tarragon, chervil)
salt and freshly ground black pepper to taste
6 fillet steaks

SAUCE
30 g (1 oz) butter
60 g (2 oz) finely chopped onions
2 tablespoons whisky
3 cups brown beef stock
1 tablespoon green peppercorns, drained and rinsed
1 tablespoon finely chopped parsley
1 tablespoon finely chopped chives

A combination of the most simple ingredients — a perfectly grilled steak in which is hidden the stuffing we have all enjoyed as children, its demi-glaze sharpened with green peppercorns and given an additional boost with whisky at the last minute.

We used this recipe at a product launch dinner for a client. We catered for 150, served everyone's steak medium-rare, and held our breath to see if anyone would return the steak to be cooked further. It didn't happen, and nothing came back uneaten.

It is a most horrible feeling, listening in that moment of silence as food is taken out. I worry just as any cook does, checking plates that come back after guests have finished their dinner, asking dining-room staff a thousand times 'did everyone like it?', staying awake into the small hours trying to improve a dish that I am not totally happy with, and living in fear that someone will one day throw their food at the wall and walk out. It hasn't happened yet, and hopefully is only a figment of this food addict's vivid imagination.

Method

To make the stuffing, sauté the onions and garlic in the butter until soft; do not brown. Add the bread cubes, toss well until all the butter is absorbed by the bread and the bread is evenly coated. Stir in the chopped herbs and season well with salt and pepper. Pocket-stuff each fillet steak (see Notes) and later grill as desired.

For the sauce, heat the butter in a saucepan until it is sizzling. Add the onions and cook until a light golden brown, about 6 minutes. Add the whisky, carefully flambé, and add the beef stock. Simmer for 20 minutes and when reduced to a light coating consistency add the peppercorns, parsley and chives. Check seasoning. The quality of the sauce will depend on the quality of the stock; if the stock is already very strong do not reduce but simmer to marry the flavours, adding water if the flavour of the stock is too rich.

Notes

When making the stuffing, season it to suit your palate but remember that the flavour of the herbs will increase with sitting. If you do not like the filling as 'dense', fold in a lightly beaten egg white, but re-season as this will knock the flavours back.

To pocket-stuff a steak is to partly slice the steak horizontally, leaving a gap or pocket to fill with the stuffing. Use a toothpick to seal the pocket if you are worried about leakage during grilling.

You can very easily grill your steak during the day, pocket-stuff it with herb stuffing and then heat it in the oven at night for your guests. When pre-grilling do it on a very high heat, and sear it quickly. The idea is to get the steak well coloured but not cooked. You are at this stage cooking it to blue, an extremely rare steak.

The sauce can be made pan style if you wish. However, I am a great believer in planning in advance, and prefer to have the sauce prepared before guests arrive. Pan sauces can be very variable and are only at their best when cooking for six or less at one time. For a pan sauce, grill the steaks and remove to the oven to hold. Add the sauce ingredients to the pan and deglaze, making use of the meat juices. This is often finished with a little slackened cornflour and a nob of butter, or reduced down to a glaze. When sauces are heavily reduced you do get a high-protein sauce which is extremely rich. I find that a very little cornflour, slackened in water and added off the heat to the sauce in tiny amounts, is all that is needed to give the sauce a light coating texture.

However you cook the sauce, it is vital that it is very thin; you should be able to see the plate through it, all the peppercorns should look like little jewels, and the herbs should be as green as green. It should be a picture of simplicity with great flavour.

Pork *with* Rosemary *and* White Wine

White Tie Catering is often asked to design theme functions — menus to suit an occasion, enriched by amazing table settings, music that complements the theme, and locations that inspire. It's exciting and always different. It upsets you, excites you and exhausts you. This recipe was designed for such an event.

The art gallery was the setting. It was an artist's fortieth birthday. She just loved pork but wanted it light. We had 60 guests with a kitchen that simply contained a water heater and a sink. Not easy! However, after playing around with flavours, from the most complicated to the 'one-stage' simple, we came up with this dish that holds well, does not dry out the pork and has sophisticated flavour and taste. This dish is even better when made up the day before, then heated for service, as the flavours mellow and develop.

We served the pork with a hot julienned salad of autumn vegetables and a galette of waxy potatoes.

½ cup golden raisins
1 cup vermouth
500 g (1 lb) pork tenderloin, cleaned of all fat and blue muscle skin
½ cup flour
30 g (1 oz) butter
1 ½ cups finely chopped onion
1 tablespoon each fresh chopped thyme and rosemary
zest of 1 orange
3 cups good jelled chicken stock
2 bayleaves
parsley stalks
2 tablespoons herbs, finely chopped (perhaps chervil, lemon thyme and marjoram)

Method

Soak the raisins overnight in the vermouth. Slice and pound out the pork into escalopes. Dust lightly in flour and sauté in butter in a hot frying pan. Once browned, put the pork to one side to remain warm. Add the onions to the pan with the thyme and rosemary. Cook until the onions are soft but not coloured. Add the vermouth, raisins, orange zest, stock, bayleaves and a few parsley stalks. Simmer until the sauce is a light coating texture. Discard the bayleaves and parsley stalks and add the fine herbs at the very last moment to maintain their colour. Serve with the pork.

Notes

When serving this dish at a function we cook the pork and chill it, create the sauce using the pork juices and chill this as well. Then it is only a matter of combining the cold pork and sauce, covering with foil and gently heating in a moderate oven. There is no reason why you cannot do this when entertaining at home.

Always be careful with meat, ensuring that it is chilled quickly as soon as cooked, and that it does not sit in the hot sauce for too long. It is always best to err on the side of caution, and if in doubt do not serve what may just have sat at room temperature a little long.

Chicken *with* Plum *and* Walnuts

1 chicken segmented into 8
1 tablespoon ketchup manis
60 g (2 oz) butter
1 tablespoon finely chopped green ginger
2 onions, finely chopped
500 g (1 lb) cooked, stoned and puréed plums
3 cups chicken stock
3 tablespoons hoisin sauce
4 tablespoons sugar
2 tablespoons cornflour, slackened with ½ cup stock
1½ cups fresh walnut halves, blanched and roasted, to garnish
chives or spring onion, to garnish

One of my great passions is books. Whenever I travel I prom ise myself I will not go into a bookshop, well not until the last days of my trip. I always succumb. Without fail I return with one, perhaps two, suitcases of books — books I just had to have. Books that may just have one recipe that caught my eye, I may love a photo, a presentation trick or simply the style of writing.

My brother Tony, a joiner who has a talent for bookcases, built a library especially for this collection, and we are now designing a two-storeyed addition that will house the overflow that has occurred. This recipe developed from sitting down in the library with numerous books open, trying to come up with an interesting variation on chicken.

I was going through one of my Asian phases at the time, and the addition of hoisin, ginger and ketchup manis reflects this; my love of Persian cooking, with its tendency towards fruit with meat, is also evident.

This recipe, like so many of my main-course recipes, can be made to order, prepared in advance, or the sauce can be created and frozen for a busier time in the week when you want to entertain. It is excellent with fresh, home-bottled or even commercially canned plums. I like to use the large, dark Black Doris or Omega plums, as they give the sauce colour, sharpness and body.

Method

Pre-heat the oven to 180°C/350°F. Brush the chicken with the ketchup manis and bake for about 25 minutes until it is crisp and barely cooked. Sauté the onions and ginger in butter until lightly coloured, about 5 minutes, add the plums and stock and simmer for 15 minutes. Add the hoisin sauce, sugar and cornflour to thicken lightly. Check the seasoning and pass the sauce through a sieve.

To serve I like to have the sauce hot, dip in the just-cooked chicken to coat it totally, then plate. Garnish with the chives and walnuts. A little orange zest would add colour and complement the flavour well.

For a good well-rounded flavour, leave the chicken sitting in the sauce for 10 minutes or so. This will mellow the sauce and lift the taste of the chicken. Meat left to rest in a sauce can only improve the finished dish. Both the chicken and the sauce should be kept hot throughout this process.

Notes

Blanch the walnuts in boiling water and dry thoroughly. Fry in a little oil until golden but be very careful as walnuts burn rapidly. Preparing them this way intensifies the walnut flavour. I store these in an airtight container in the freezer.

Always buy ginger when it is just fresh in at the market. It should feel smooth and glossy, heavy and firm. Buy more than you need, scrape the ginger and keep the peelings stored in dry sherry; when it has matured after a couple of weeks, use it to enrich sauces; store the cleaned ginger in sherry, vodka or a light sugar syrup in the fridge. Nothing should ever go to waste and this gives you access to excellent ginger and ginger spirits or syrups throughout the year.

When it has aged, ginger is shrivelled, woody and light in weight; it can ruin a recipe by becoming acrid as it sits in a dish.

We also store juniper berries in sherry. This creates a great essence for game cooking, for terrine work and for lifting a soup or sauce that is 'thin' in flavour.

MIGHTY MAINS

Chicken *with* Yoghurt *and* Red Pepper Coulis

It took my day chef, Ann, and me a whole day of cooking, tasting and cooking again to come up with this recipe. We wanted something light and summery, we wanted a recipe that would keep the chicken breast moist, but we did not want a heavy, cloying sauce.

MIGHTY MAINS

It consists of whole boned chicken breasts that are filled with a yoghurt, herb and apple stuffing, which is carefully placed under the skin of each breast. This method works well with a variety of fillings. The filling can be made well in advance and the breasts can be stuffed and frozen or stuffed the day before and baked or roasted several hours before serving. Though best served hot from the oven, they can be reheated successfully. They are wonderful sliced and served chilled at a picnic or, if not held too long, delicious served at room temperature with a salad of warm sautéed lettuce.

The red pepper coulis is one of the few sauces I make that uses commercial chicken stock, the powdered variety. Homemade stock, as good as it is, colours the coulis and does not give it the salts it requires. Perhaps it is that tiny amount of MSG that is needed.

60 g (2 oz) natural yoghurt
60 g (2 oz) cottage cheese
zest and juice of 1 lemon
2 tablespoons finely chopped parsley
2 tablespoons finely chopped marjoram
1 small onion, finely chopped
½ cup cooked, finely chopped apple
soft white breadcrumbs to bind, about ½ cup
salt and pepper to taste
8 chicken breasts
apple juice (optional)
butter (optional)

Method

Preheat the oven to 180°C/350°F.

Process the yoghurt, cottage cheese and lemon juice until smooth. Add the herbs, onion, apple, lemon zest and breadcrumbs to bind. Check seasoning. Gently stuff under the skin of the breasts. Tuck the skin and meat underneath to form a rounded shape and bake for 25 minutes.

Serve with a pool of red pepper coulis and a tiny salad of baby garden-fresh greens.

I like to make a mixture of apple juice and butter and brush the breast with this before I cook it. The additional bite of the apple just seems to lift the flavour. The breast can also be laid in a tray and poached in approximately 1 cm (½ in) of stock. This helps to keep the breast moist, although the colour is a tad bland. You might like then to grill the skin quickly to colour it, or use a blow-torch as many professional chefs do.

Red Pepper *Coulis*

Combine all the ingredients except the cornflour and simmer until the peppers are soft; blend and check seasoning. Reheat and thicken with a little cornflour to give substance. Store in a container in the refrigerator until needed. The coulis can be served hot or cold.

Substitute yellow peppers for a yellow coulis and increase the sugar a little. Do check seasoning.

2 red peppers, seeded and diced
1½ cups chicken stock
2 tablespoons malt or balsamic vinegar
1–2 teaspoons brown sugar
slackened cornflour to thicken

Notes

Peach schnapps is the most exquisite liqueur. If you have some of this, a splash in the sauce at the last minute will lift the dish into another world. For me a generous nip of peach schnapps in the bottom of a tall champagne flute, topped up with well-chilled champagne, would be just perfect to go with the chicken. In fact, peach schnapps and champagne is just perfect for anything, from breakfast to late supper.

Little Chickens *in* Sauternes

The idea of serving whole baby chickens will not be to everyone's taste, but my students had been asking for weeks for a recipe for these creatures, and I came up with this.

Again, my love for fruit with meat comes to the fore, but by no means do you need to stick to this. Peaches are not always in season, but little chickens are. Try yams, crab apples, or perhaps beets. Whatever you do use, try to get some of that flavour into the stuffing. For example, caramelise some yams on the top of the stove with a little honey and vinegar, purée and add it to the breadcrumbs; the flavour will carry right through the dish.

Method

Preheat the oven to 180°C/350°F.

Cut the peaches in half and remove the stones. Place them on a roasting tray, sprinkle with brown sugar and roast until well coloured and soft. Take one peach and chop it finely. Put the remaining peaches to one side.

Combine the breadcrumbs, onion, 2 tablespoons of thyme, 2 tablespoons of the butter and the finely chopped peach and season to taste. Divide into six and fill the chickens. There is no need to truss the chickens and they should only be loosely stuffed, allowing the stuffing to swell.

Heat the frying pan with butter and oil, and brown the birds. Pack them breast side down into a roasting dish with the bayleaf, thyme and peppercorns. Pour over a bottle of Sauternes and the stock. Roast, basting regularly to keep moist, and taking care not to overcook. They should be ready within 30 minutes but this will depend on how tightly they are packed in the tray.

Drain the juices into a small saucepan with the slackened cornflour. Bring to a simmer and pour over the chickens. Serve the chickens garnished with the roasted peach and fresh thyme.

7 fresh peaches, blanched and skinned
3 tablespoons brown sugar
6 small chickens, preferably size 0
3 cups fresh white breadcrumbs
2 onions, finely chopped
4 tablespoons thyme leaves
6 tablespoons butter
2 tablespoons oil
1 bayleaf
8 peppercorns
1 bottle Sauternes
4 cups chicken stock
1 tablespoon cornflour, slackened with 1 tablespoon water
thyme for garnish

MIGHTY MAINS

'A *cook* or a chef *who* knows it all *should* really *consider* changing *jobs*.'

disgraceful desserts

Lemon Syllabub Torte *142*
Akaroa Walnut Tart with Green Grape Glaze *144*
Persian Meringue Cake with Stained Glass Sugar *146*
Polenta Pudding with Blackberry Compôte and Mascarpone Cream *148*
Oranges in Champagne with Toffeed Strawberries *150*
White Chocolate Cake Soufflé with Tangerine Sauce *152*
Coconut Cake with Warm Conserve *154*
Steeped Oranges with Green Ginger *156*
Cappucino Ice Cream with Spooned Walnut Brûlée *158*
Butterscotch Sauce *160*
Sherried Fruit Sauce *160*

*F*or me there are two major problems with being in the food business — being overdrawn at the bank and overweight in the body. I can ignore the overdraft by giving it all to my accountant to worry about, but for the life of me I cannot ignore being overweight. I try to cut down. I attempt to have breakfast, eat lots of rabbit fodder and cut down on the alcohol, but when a dessert is placed in front of me I indulge with gusto. Obviously I enjoy eating — I savour the flavours of canapés, discuss the consistency of soup, ramble on about the moist breast of chicken, but I anticipate the moment for dessert with glee. In front of me sits this wonderful-looking morsel and suddenly I think, why throw away something that someone has gone to so much trouble to make, and something that will give me such happiness?

Dessert surely is the part of the meal where people indulge themselves and throw caution to the winds. A glimpse of a creamy

◦ DISGRACEFUL DESSERTS

gâteau, syllabub or pastry often banishes all thoughts of eating healthily and sensibly. But all is not lost, just tell yourself you will go for an extra long jog tomorrow and the feeling of guilt will disappear; promise yourself an extra hour at the gym when you ask for a second helping. Surely guilt should never get in the way of a good dessert.

On a more serious note, if we ate rich desserts all the time they wouldn't be such a pleasure, and it is only truly possible to enjoy a rich dessert if the rest of the meal is well balanced. All desserts do not contain cream, eggs and sugar. Exquisite desserts can be created that are light, refreshing and non-fattening, that are innovative and taste wonderful.

The most important point about a dessert is that it is often the finale of a meal, so it should be something worthy of remembrance, something that will linger on the tastebuds of your guests and make them want to taste it again. Whether it is a healthy creation of fresh orange with cardamom and ginger, or a rich creamy brûlée finished with Sauternes, it should complement the total meal, have great colour, texture, and most importantly, flavour.

Smells are like scrapbook notes in the mind, and to me the smells of desserts bring forth so many memories. The smell of sweet baked apples always reminds me of Mrs Stevens who, when anything went wrong in our family, would rush down a large apple sponge to comfort us. The smell of fruit cakes baking conjures up the tradition of the six of us taking turns at stirring the large Christmas cake. The smell of cinnamon reminds me of mulled wine and our much-loved winter parties, and the heavenly smell of lemon honey being made, later to be layered between meringue, always reminds me of Jessica, my great-grandmother who was citrus-mad.

'In *front* of me sits this *wonderful*-looking morsel and *suddenly* I think, why throw away something that someone has *gone* to so much *trouble* to make, and *something* that will *give* me *such* happiness?'

Lemon Syllabub Torte

Olive was my tower of strength in maintaining the foodies group that dined at Michael's Restaurant once a month, she encouraged me to set up the Small Kitchen School, and she pushed me harder and harder to achieve higher standards, not only in food and presentation but in recipe testing and wine tasting. She was 60, had more energy than most people half her age and boy, did she just love pudding. We designed this dessert for her. Olive loved lemon almost as much as feijoas, which were her passion. In fact, I am more than certain she tried this recipe with feijoa jam, cream and Cognac. Olive and I worked on a recipe using overripe pink gooseberries with the syllabub and found the combination just perfect. We found it so wonderful that we sat down with a bottle of champagne and ate the entire torte.

Smooth, creamy and ethereal, this exquisitely elegant torte is an instant favourite with any citrus lover. The moist genoise, the bite of the lemon enriched with white wine and finished with cream, all go to create a dessert that is just perfect for entertaining. The torte is a caterer's dream. It can be prepared well in advance, in fact it is often better left a few days before eating, it holds well when left in its tin and will still be perfect a week after being made. It is wonderful accompanied by thinly sliced citron, with lemon glazed in a syrup, with a light orange salad, or simply served with lightly whipped cream and a sprig of mint or lemon balm.

You can either make the genoise sponge cake yourself or buy it in. Whichever you use, it is best that the sponge is at least two days old, and make sure you remove the outside skin of the sponge; there should be no tan colour left at all. We cut it off with a bread knife and dust the cake with a brush to remove all the crumbs. Slice the cake into layers of about 1 cm (½ in), or as thin as the cake will slice before it crumbles. Put the sponge to one side and make up the syllabub.

Genoise

3 tablespoons clarified unsalted butter
1 teaspoon vanilla extract
4 large eggs
½ cup sugar
½ cup sifted flour
⅓ cup cornflour

A genoise is a European sponge-type cake which differs from many sponges in that it contains butter to tenderise and flavour it, and much less sugar. It is great in this recipe as even when the syrup is added the sponge is not overly sweet. This is one of the few recipes that I measure exactly. I have the eggs at room temperature and work quickly once the eggs are beaten so that they do not deflate. The flour is folded in with a gentle hand and once thoroughly mixed I put the cake into the oven immediately. Having cooked in numerous ovens, I find that they all differ, so you may need to adjust the temperature to suit your oven.

DISGRACEFUL DESSERTS

Citrus Fruits

Combine 2 cups of sugar and 1 cup of water in a pot and bring to the boil. Add thinly sliced citrus fruits to this and boil until the fruits are just beginning to go opaque, or until when you put a spoon into the mixture and hold it up, the syrup forms a sheet as it falls. Be careful not to overboil, as the fruits can become bitter. The citrus fruits I use are oranges, lemons, limes and grapefruit. The fruit is sliced, skin and all, and the amount used is just enough to be covered by the syrup. It is a very easy recipe and can be stored in airtight jars for several months.

Method

Preheat the oven to 160°C/325°F. Line the bottom of a round 21 cm (9 in) tin with paper; grease and flour the tin.

Put a small bowl in warm water and add the butter and vanilla extract; leave to gently melt. Sift the flour and cornflour onto waxed paper and put to one side.

Place the eggs and sugar in a large mixing bowl that is being kept warm in a water bath or the sink. Mix well to prevent the sugar 'cooking' the eggs. With a hand-held electric beater, beat the eggs and sugar until they have tripled in volume. Remove 3 tablespoons of this mixture and add it to the melted butter and vanilla.

Sprinkle half the flour into the remaining egg mixture, fold in gently but thoroughly, and add the remaining flour mixture. I use a large rubber spatula for folding the flour in. Next fold in the butter mixture until it is barely folded through. Pour into the prepared tin and cook in the oven for about 30 minutes, until the cake is golden and coming away from the sides. Once cooked remove from the oven, loosen the sides of the cake with a knife and unmould at once onto a lightly greased cake rack. Cool and store until needed.

Syllabub

Put the wine, lemon juice, rind and sugar in a bowl and leave for at least 3 hours. Stir at intervals, making sure all the sugar is dissolved. Add the cream to the mixture and slowly whip it until the mixture will hold its shape.

Line a loaf tin or similar with plastic wrap, leaving a good 15 cm (6 in) hanging over the sides. Slice the sponge to fit; do not worry about patchworking it as this will not show. Lay a slice of sponge on the base of the tin, spread 3 tablespoons of the syllabub mixture on top, and repeat the process until the tin is filled. Add another layer of sponge to come over the top of the tin and cover with the plastic wrap. Put the torte in the refrigerator and weight it overnight. The longer it is left the better. Wine may separate from the syllabub and when this happens simply turn the torte upside down and the liquid will run back through the sponge.

Turn the torte out, cut it with a hot knife and serve with lightly whipped cream. I like to use citrus fruits with this torte, with a small amount of the syrup from the fruits around the torte, but a simple strawberry can look just as magical.

4 tablespoons white wine
1 tablespoon lemon juice
1 teaspoon grated lemon rind
½ cup castor sugar
¾ cup cream

Akaroa Walnut Tart *with* Green Grape Glaze

We have in New Zealand some of the best produce in the world, and Akaroa walnuts are a perfect example. Planted by the French when they settled in the early 1800s, these walnut trees produce the most moreish, well-flavoured walnuts possible.

This recipe is the crème de la crème of tarts, for it makes the most of these walnuts, the flavour being in both the pastry and the filling. Make sure the walnuts you use are fresh, for rancid walnuts, even a single one in this recipe, will give you a most unpleasant flavour. If you are unsure, lightly toasting the walnuts may help.

This tart is also superb made with hazelnuts and almonds.

Pastry

200 g (6 oz) butter
125 g (4 oz) icing sugar
1 large egg
1 teaspoon lemon juice
90 g (3 oz) finely ground walnuts
300 g (10 oz) plain flour

Preheat the oven to 200°C/400°F. Cream the butter and sugar together until pale. Beat in the egg, add the lemon juice and ground walnuts, and finally the flour. Mix to a smooth paste and rest in the refrigerator for at least 30 minutes.

Roll out the pastry on a floured surface and place in a greased 20 cm (8 in) tart tin. Prick the base, bake for 10 minutes, then allow to cool. We prefer to use metal tart tins as porcelain containers are inclined to hold the heat and take longer to cook and cool. The base will be cooked again so at this stage we are only setting the pastry and trying not to colour it too much.

Filling

125 g (4 oz) coarsely ground walnuts
125 g (4 oz) castor sugar
30 g (1 oz) icing sugar
1 egg white, beaten

Mix all the ingredients together. Spoon into the cool tart base and reheat in a lower oven (180°C/350°F) for about 30 minutes, or until the walnut filling is set. If the pastry colours too fast, place foil around the edges to protect it.

Green *Grape* Glaze

Gently heat the conserve until it is just melted. Purée in a blender and pass through a sieve. Fold in the champagne liqueur and brush over the tart before it cools.

½ cup green grape conserve
1 tablespoon champagne liqueur

Serve the tart in wedges with cream enriched with champagne liqueur and sweetened slightly.

DISGRACEFUL DESSERTS

Notes

This tart is excellent whatever temperature you serve it at. It stores well and is delightful served with a vanilla ice cream that has been enriched with either a splash of Baileys Irish Cream or had some strong black coffee folded through.

Use almonds instead of walnuts and accompany the tart with some warm grapes that have been sautéed with a little butter and a shot of brandy.

Persian Meringue Cake *with* Stained-Glass Sugar

This Persian meringue cake is an adaptation of a cake taught to me by Gretta Anna Teplitzky, the founder of Australia's first cooking schools. A talented teacher, her classes have been almost completely booked out for the last 25 years. This cake is an indication of her talent.

An upmarket meringue cake, it is rich, simple and inexpensive. I have cooked this cake so often I am sure I can do it in my sleep. It is the ultimate in make-ahead desserts; we have found that the unfilled cake can be made, chilled and wrapped in plastic wrap, and left in a cool cupboard for up to two months. It is simply heaven for last-minute entertaining, for trying to look talented, smart and organised when all you had to do was whip the cream, add stained glass sugar for extra elegance if you wish, leaving you with plenty of time to put your hair up and relax with a gin.

The food of Iran is delicate, gently seasoned and fragrant with the most aromatic of spices and with the essences of citrus fruits and flowers. Almonds, rosewater and citrus peel are all ingredients used frequently in Persian cooking. I have taken the liberty of adding chocolate to this recipe. I use white chocolate, but only because it is my favourite; dark or milk chocolate are perfectly suitable.

Meringue Cake

4 egg whites
250 g (8 oz) castor sugar
125 g (4 oz) coarsely chopped chocolate
90 g (3 oz) mixed peel
125 g (4 oz) blanched almonds, chopped
90 g (3 oz) crystallised ginger, finely chopped

Preheat the oven to 160°C/325°F. Line the base of a 20 cm (8 in) springform tin with baking paper. The sides of the tin do not need to be greased.

Beat the egg whites until stiff, then beat in the sugar. Add all the other ingredients, fold together and spoon into the prepared tin. Bake for 35 minutes. The cake will go golden brown and puff up in the middle. If you are putting a skewer in to check if it is cooked, remember the chocolate will be liquid, so do not bake until it is totally dry. I bake until the cake is golden and slightly withdrawn from the sides. Once cooked, take it out of the oven and gently push the top of the cake in to leave you with a large hollow in the centre. When cooled the cake can be wrapped in plastic and stored until needed.

Filling

300 ml (½ pint) cream, lightly whipped
½ teaspoon rosewater
2 tablespoons icing sugar

Whip the cream with the rosewater and sugar. Fill the hollow of the cake generously and stand the stained-glass sugar up in the cream.

Notes

When working with sugar and such heat as in the stained-glass sugar, always have a bowl of cold water nearby, use only dry towels to remove the tray from the oven, and make sure no children are around. It is a very simple and elegant addition to the cake, but if you feel unsure about doing it, the cake will still look great.

The meringue is best filled with the cream an hour before being served. This softens the meringue and gives a very pleasant texture. Once the shafts are added it is best served within the hour.

Individual cakes can be made in muffin tins; cook for a shorter time and store individually wrapped in a container.

This is a most versatile cake. Pistachios can of course be used, and look great; I have made it with chocolate, with walnuts, and with dried pawpaw, pineapple, apricot and mango. Make it with more ginger, omit the citrus peel and serve it with lightly whipped cream laced with Kirsch and topped with white-chocolate-dipped strawberries.

Create a total citrus meringue cake, replacing the chocolate, almonds and ginger with equal amounts of peel. Fill the middle with segments of oranges drizzled with Grand Marnier and decorated with sugared cardamom. Consider making orange honey, fold some into yoghurt and cream whipped together and fill the cake generously with this. The variations are limitless.

Stained-Glass Sugar

Turn your grill onto full. Cover a heavy oven tray with foil and brush the foil with oil. Sprinkle the sugar unevenly over the foil. Place under the grill and wait until the sugar has begun to melt; watch it carefully as all grills are different and some may only take 30 seconds while others may take 2 minutes. Parts will discolour more than others and some will not melt completely. Do not worry, this is the effect we need. Remove from the grill and put to one side for the sugar to set. Once cooled, lift the sugar up; it will have formed a sheet and look like stained glass. Crack into uneven shafts and stand these up in the cream. It is beautiful with edible gold dust sprinkled on the sugar as soon as it is removed from the oven.

This can be made well in advance and stored in an airtight container. If damp gets in, the glass sugar will begin to melt.

1 teaspoon oil
½ cup sugar

Polenta Pudding *with* Blackberry Compôte *and* Mascarpone Cream

This is one of the desserts I use in the cooking school to distinguish between simple desserts and a pastry chef's complex, time-consuming constructions. Such fancy celebration cakes require endless time and patience, and you have to remove everything else from the fridge and station a guard to protect them from poachers. As hard as you work you will have no idea what your cake tastes like until you cut into it, and that just may be too late.

I am not trying to discourage the class from tackling sophisticated cakes. I just want them to note that the rewards from cooking a good, simple dessert come more easily than from a fussy dessert.

I will never forget the effort I went to for a very special dinner party of friends, making the most amazing dessert, only to find that they were all watching their weight and the no longer slim dog ate the majority. Soul destroying!

Hot and cold, sweet and acid, this simple pudding is not only very modern in its use of polenta and mascarpone, but it is the most straightforward dish to create. It warms your heart, makes your lips pucker, and transports you to fantasies of cosy evenings in front of large log fires. Although made in three stages, they are all very simple and can be prepared well in advance.

Polenta Cake

Preheat the oven to 160°C/325°F. Lightly grease a 30 cm (12 in) cake tin and put to one side.

Beat the butter, sugar and vanilla seeds in an electric mixer until creamy. Beat in the eggs and egg yolks one at a time. Fold in the polenta and flour and pour into the prepared tin. Bake for 1¼ hours. Unmould the cake onto a rack and let it cool.

1½ cups soft butter
5 cups icing sugar
seeds from ¼ vanilla bean
4 eggs
2 egg yolks
1 cup polenta
2 cups flour

Berry *Compôte*

Combine the berries and sugar and cook gently until the sugar is dissolved and the berries have broken down. Cool and add the Kirsch if desired.

6 cups blackberries, fresh or frozen
¾ cup sugar
3 tablespoons Kirsch (optional)

Marscapone *Cream*

125 g (4 oz) mascarpone
250 g (8 oz) cream
45 g (1½ oz) sugar

Simply whip all to a soft peak and reserve until ready to use. Hold in the fridge, covered.

To serve, place the cake in a larger cake pan and pour over two-thirds of the berry compôte, juices and all, and leave the cake to sit overnight to soak up the mixture. Slice the cake into wedges, reheat it in a low oven and serve it warm. I like to heat the compôte and serve it poured over the cake. Top with a dollop of mascarpone cream and you're at the threshold of foodies' heaven.

Oranges *in* Champagne *with* Toffeed Strawberries

We all dream of those picture-perfect desserts that draw oohs, aahs and applause. This is one that is miles easier than it looks, and it can be prepared well in advance of a dinner party. However, I would not attempt the strawberries on a hot, humid day as the toffee will simply go to syrup. This is a wonderfully festive dessert, which sings of summer and the sun. The combination of oranges, strawberries and champagne is elegant, colourful yet not too rich. Of course you do not want to use the very best vintage champagne, but do not skimp either. Remember a dish cannot be any better than the quality of its ingredients — the oranges must have good flavour and the strawberries be sun-ripened.

When shopping for the fruit for this I often take a knife, buy one orange, slice it into quarters and taste it there and then. I do the same with the strawberries as it avoids the problem of getting home to discover the fruit is not suitable for this recipe.

8 oranges
4 teaspoons gelatine
150 ml ¼ pint) orange juice
250 ml (8 fl oz) champagne
2 tablespoons castor sugar
mint leaves (optional)
2 punnets strawberries
2 cups sugar
2 tablespoons glucose
½ cup water

Method

Peel the oranges, removing all the pith, and segment them, saving all the juice. Pat the segments dry and hold to one side.

Sprinkle the gelatine over 3 tablespoons of orange juice and put aside to sponge, or soften. Put the 150 ml (¼ pint) orange juice in a small pot and add the champagne, sugar and sponged gelatine. Gently heat until all the gelatine is dissolved. Remove from the heat and chill until the mixture becomes syrupy.

Brush six moulds with some of the syrup and arrange mint leaves on the bottom, having the points well out to the edge. Layer orange segments in the moulds, pouring a little orange syrup between each layer. Fill to the top of the mould and pour in the remaining syrup. Tap the moulds to remove all the air bubbles and chill.

Place the sugar, glucose and water in a small pot and simmer until dissolved. Increase the heat slightly and as soon as the syrup begins to colour dip the strawberries in, holding them by the stem. Sit to one side for the toffeed sugar to set.

Turn out the moulds onto the middle of large mains-sized plates and pile the toffee strawberries on top. Serve straight away. I like to serve this with a bowl of yoghurt enriched with a small amount of plain lightly whipped cream. It's a glorious combination and cuts the richness of the toffee.

Notes

The strawberries are a garnish trick and one well worth playing around with. Again be careful and only do these when you are relaxed, and have cold water and damp towels on hand in case of mishap. When we first did these we put a large kebab skewer through each strawberry, dipped it in the toffee and laid the dripping strawberry across a bowl to let the toffee slowly drip and leave a long thread on the fruit.

The toffee can be reheated as you work if it becomes too firm, but be careful not to burn the sugar or the toffee fruit will be bitter.

Again this is one of those wonderful recipes that you can chop and change to suit the seasons and availability of fruit. The main thing is to have flavours that complement each other — peach in champagne with toffeed strawberries, strawberries in champagne with toffeed green grapes, mango with lime is a classic (set the mango in the champagne and dip lime segments in the toffee) and kiwifruit in champagne with toffeed crystallised ginger is exquisite.

When dipping fruit in toffee make sure the fruit is dry before dipping or the sugar may spit. With the exception of strawberries, most berries are too liquid, so be very careful when first trying them.

DISGRACEFUL DESSERTS

White Chocolate Cake Soufflé *with* Tangerine Sauce

I always thought white chocolate was not as fattening as dark; it looked lighter somehow, and I assumed it had no wicked tendency to add more padding to my tummy. I ate it with enthusiasm, then discovered that it actually has more calories than dark chocolate. Nevertheless I simply adore white chocolate, its creamy texture, the way it melts in your mouth and that wonderful flavour. Anything on a menu with white chocolate, I would order. I created recipes just for my addiction. I found that by adding vermouth when melting it for a mousse it still had the magic and was nowhere near as rich, hence we could incorporate the mousse into restaurant menus. I added white chocolate to shortbread, created the most crisp white chocolate base for a white chocolate cheese cake that had edible gold folded through, and found that a white chocolate and gooseberry ice cream was sublime. If I could I would add white chocolate to just about anything, simply to get my fix.

This recipe is one I particularly enjoy as it has the lightness of a soufflé, the sharpness of the tangerine sauce, and that lovable white chocolate. It is a great recipe for entertaining, making you look very professional, for the soufflé has tangerine sauce poured into it and therefore does not have to be perfect. If it is a disaster, pour in more sauce to give more height, have some curls of white chocolate on hand, place them on top of the warm soufflé, and dust it with icing sugar. What could be nicer? Serve additional sauce in a jug so that guests can pour more as they please.

Soufflé

Preheat the oven to 180°C/350°F. Prepare the ramekins (1-cup size), rubbing butter over the sides and bottoms and sprinkling with sugar, tilting them to coat the sides.

3 tablespoons soft unsalted butter
125 g (4 oz) white chocolate, grated
2 tablespoons milk
5½ tablespoons sugar, plus additional for sprinkling in the ramekins
3 egg yolks
1 teaspoon good vanilla extract
4 egg whites
icing sugar to dust

DISGRACEFUL DESSERTS

Be sure not to miss any areas. Shake out the excess sugar.

Melt the white chocolate in the top of a double-boiler and stir in the milk and 4 tablespoons of sugar. Mix gently but thoroughly. Remove from the heat and allow to cool for 5 minutes. Add the egg yolks, beating constantly. Stir in the vanilla.

Whip the egg whites together until they form stiff peaks, adding the remaining 1½ tablespoons sugar halfway through. Stir one-third of the whites into the yolks then fold in the remaining whites until all are incorporated. Fill the ramekins almost to the brim with the soufflé mixture and bake in the centre of the oven until puffed and brown. I find this takes about 15 minutes.

Tangerine Sauce

¾ cup tangerine or orange juice
2 teaspoons Grand Marnier
2 tablespoons sugar
2 teaspoons arrowroot or cornflour
½ cup tangerine segments, chopped coarsely

While the soufflés are baking prepare the tangerine sauce. Combine the juice, Grand Marnier, sugar and arrowroot in a small saucepan. Simmer, stirring constantly, for 4 minutes and add the tangerine pieces.

Have your plates ready, icing sugar sitting to one side in a small sieve, and white chocolate curls on a plate just in case they are needed. Remove the soufflés from the oven, place on the plates and, making a hole in the centre of each one, pour in a little hot sauce. Place a few curls on top of the soufflé and dust both soufflé and plate generously with icing sugar. Serve immediately and just accept the praise with style.

Notes

Tangerines are also called clementines. If they are not available, blood oranges, also called sanguines, would be wonderful. Really any good well-flavoured member of the orange family will do. I have made this recipe using tangerine marmalade thinned out with a splash of orange juice, so nothing is impossible.

Grating white chocolate helps it to melt without going lumpy. I now always grate chocolate before melting it. Use a good white chocolate — if you are going to eat food that is fattening, you may as well truly enjoy it.

The difference between chocolates is quite significant and I often have to sit down with several makes and have a tasting session just to make sure I haven't forgotten. I recommend this recipe with white, milk and dark chocolate, but not on the same day.

I always use white china ramekins for baking soufflés. I find they hold the heat longer when on the table, preventing the soufflé collapsing too fast. Another hint is always to eat a soufflé from the middle out, as this will prevent it from collapsing straight away.

I often make up this soufflé, put the mix into the ramekins and place them in the fridge until needed. I have made these three hours in advance, and slipped them into the oven just before the mains were cleared. It is significant that the soufflé is the only dish that guests should wait for, other than a good risotto perhaps; the soufflé should not wait for the guests.

Coconut Cake *with* Warm Conserve

Although I dislike dark chocolate I still enjoy macaroons. Have you ever tried to eat the coconut filling out of a chocolate macaroon? It's definitely something you do in the privacy of your own home. This recipe is a coconut-lover's dream come true. A most angelic cake, with a soft, moist filling, a subtle wrapping of pastry and the piquant bite of a warm conserve. It is the most simple of desserts to put together yet it offers extraordinary results.

This is a good example of how recipes are created. The filling, with the addition of vanilla-enriched sugar and citrus rind, came from my sister Virginia's much-loved collection of fattening foods. The idea of pastry was suggested by my good friend Donald, who constantly suggests I diet, or else put on more weight so he can stand close by and look younger and much thinner. Some friends are just like that. 'Why not,' he said, 'make it totally wicked and add pastry?' And sure as can be, that was just the most wonderful idea. We tried different sorts of pastry, from phyllo, short crust and coconut pastry to flaky, but commercial puff pastry gave the best result by far. The cake takes ten minutes to put together and is so wonderfully decadent you only need a small slice. Best made to age a few days, the rich creamy coconut filling just seems to intensify with sitting. Again, like so many of my desserts, not for a weight watcher, unless of course you have nothing but water for the next two days. It is well worth the sacrifice.

Method

Roll the pastry out and line the bottom and sides of a 20 cm (8 in) springform tin that has been buttered and floured. Chill well. Preheat the oven to 180°C/350°F.

Beat the eggs until they are beginning to foam, beat in the sugar gradually, and continue beating until very thick and light. It is most important not to underbeat. Blend in the zest, coconut and butter. Pour into the pastry case. Turn the oven down to 150°C/300°F and bake for about 50 minutes, or until a skewer comes out dry. Cool the cake slightly and remove it from the tin.

When completely cool, store the cake in plastic wrap, or an airtight tin, out of the fridge. It is best served at room temperature.

To serve, cut the cake into wedges and place a spoonful of warm conserve over and beside the cake. Serve with a side dish of plain yoghurt.

Notes

If you do not have vanilla sugar, add 1½ teaspoons of good vanilla extract at the same time as the coconut.

It is a snap to make your own vanilla sugar. It is best to use just the pods, scraping out the seeds for another use. The pods do not have much flavour on their own but when stored with sugar they infuse it with a rich vanilla scent and flavour. I store one pod to one cup of sugar, putting the sugar into airtight jars and leaving them for several weeks for the pods to infuse. At the restaurant we have a large jar that all empty pods are placed in, more sugar being added as we go. The ultimate in no-waste economy. My mother would be proud.

A good homemade apricot conserve is ideal for this recipe, but any favourite would do. If you are using a commercial conserve do check it first, and heat it with a little Cognac or fresh fruit juice to give it a lift and make it your own.

250 g (8 oz) puff pastry
4 large eggs
1½ cups castor sugar infused with vanilla (see Notes)
zest of an orange and a lemon
5 cups coconut
15 g (½ oz) butter, melted
apricot or other homemade fruit conserve

⋅❧⋅ DISGRACEFUL DESSERTS

Apricot Lemon *Conserve* with Almonds

The conserve I often serve with this cake is an apricot conserve spiked with lemon. It is an excellent winter conserve, as dried apricots are used to get a good intense flavour.

Method

Rinse the apricots, place them in a bowl and cover with water; leave overnight.

Drain, reserving the liquid. Chop the apricots and put them in a pot with the lemon. Add sugar, 4 cups of reserved liquid, and orange juice if more liquid is needed. Bring to a gentle simmer and cook for half an hour, stirring frequently. Remove from the heat, add the almonds and brandy, place in clean hot jars and seal. I always turn the jars upside down, which gives me fewer failures in the sealing.

Notes

If you don't wish to use alcohol, fruit juice is always the best substitute. In this recipe use good freshly squeezed orange juice.

1 kg (2 lb) dried apricots
2 unpeeled lemons, coarsely chopped
1½ kg (3 lb) sugar
1 cup almonds, lightly roasted and chopped
⅓ cup brandy
orange juice if needed

'Have you ever *tried* to eat the *coconut* filling out of a *chocolate* macaroon? It's definitely something you do *in the* privacy of your own *home*.'

Steeped Oranges *with* Green Ginger

A dessert that is just perfect for formal entertaining in summer or winter, for a summer lunch, a family dinner, or a relaxed light evening tea.

My mother was a dab hand at making great crêpes. She would tackle the job always on a Sunday, when this would be our evening meal, a great excuse to clean out the fridge, to get rid of all the leftovers from the week and feed six hungry children. We would all take turns at flipping, having crêpes all over the place, and as hard as we worked it seemed to take forever to accumulate a good stack. My father had a tradition of holding a penny in one hand, the crêpe pan in the other and making a wish. You would tilt the pan and give it a quick jerk and if the crêpe flipped over perfectly your wish would come true. When we had finally finished, the pile of crêpes would be put in the middle of the table and a variety of fillings were placed around. This was a wonderful family meal and although we were never allowed to raise our voices, the table was a hum of talking and activity.

Oranges were our luxury. Bought by the case and stored in the woodshed, they were one of the few fruits my mother could not grow, and one she liked us to eat. Sliced oranges in sweetened fruit juice were often served as an evening dessert, and with a few additions it was rehashed for Sunday tea. I have added my Persian flavours and come up with something a little more sophisticated. I still serve it in crêpes, but have served it also in tall, chilled champagne flutes as a finish to a formal dinner. Toasted pistachios, coarsely chopped, look summery and stunning as a garnish.

Crêpes

1¼ cups flour
4 eggs
1 cup milk
1¼ cups water
3 tablespoons butter
1 tablespoon sugar

In a blender or food processor, mix all the ingredients at high speed for 30 seconds. Scrape down the sides and blend for another 30 seconds. Pour the batter into a jug and leave to sit for at least an hour.

Heat the crêpe pan, and with a kitchen towel dipped in a small amount of melted butter and oil mixed, wipe out the pan. Pour in a small ladle of batter, swirl around and drain off any excess. The crêpe pan should have a very thin coating of batter. Cook until the mixture bubbles and is lightly coloured. Turn over and cook the other side in the same way. Turn out onto a clean towel and repeat until all the batter is finished. These can be held warm in the oven, or place a small piece of waxed paper between each crêpe and freeze for later use.

Notes

The oranges on their own are exquisite and they will hold for three days before losing any of their flavour. When they are too old to eat on their own, drain them, toss them with brown sugar and roast, serving hot on vanilla-bean ice cream. Alternatively drain, wrap in phyllo pastry, bake, and serve hot with a custard made from adding extra milk and a dash of Grand Marnier to the brûlée custard (see p.158) and cooking it in a double boiler. The syrup can be made and stored in the fridge, to warm and pour over fruit at a later stage. Grapes, melon and fresh peach are lifted into something quite magical by being stored for a good three hours in the syrup, drained and served with little homemade coconut biscuits, perhaps a citrus cream or sugared mint.

The syrup makes an excellent base for champagne. Pour a tablespoon into the bottom of a flute and top up with champagne. It's great for a brunch or a cocktail party. Using orange juice instead of champagne creates the most heavenly and refreshing drink.

Steeped Oranges

Peel the oranges and segment them, removing all trace of membrane. Put to one side. Bring a small pot of water to the boil and blanch the zest for 30 seconds. Drain and hold to one side.

In a pot bring the sugar and water to the boil. Put the cardamom and allspice in a coffee filter and tie with string. Put this in the water and simmer for 15 minutes. Add the lemon juice, citric acid and cream of tartar. Add the ginger to the syrup with the orange zest and continue to simmer for another half hour. Cool the liquid slightly and pour it over the oranges along with the Cointreau. Leave the spice bag in the syrup to steep.

Drain the oranges and wrap in the crêpes, dust generously with icing sugar, serve with a dollop of sweetened yoghurt and enjoy.

12 oranges, washed and zested
600 ml (1 pint) water
375 g (12 oz) sugar
18 cardamom pods, lightly crushed
10 whole allspice, lightly crushed
juice of 2 lemons
¼ teaspoon citric acid
½ teaspoon cream of tartar
3 cm (7 in) ginger, peeled and thinly sliced
½ cup Cointreau (optional)
icing sugar

Cappuccino Ice Cream *with* Spooned Walnut Brûlée

During one of my discussions with Lyn Hall in London the subject of walnuts and coffee came up. I have always loved our cappuccino ice cream, although possibly it should more correctly be called a parfait, and I adore crème brûlée. The thought of adding walnuts to the brûlée, cooking it in a large dish and simply spooning it to one side of the cappuccino ice cream seemed the most natural thing to do. At Michaels Restaurant we serve the ice cream in a little demi-tasse cup, the brûlée to one side and walnut pralines to add a little something extra. A touch of bitter butterscotch sauce draws the entire dish together. The walnut pralines and butterscotch are not absolutely necessary, but the brûlée and ice cream combined create a gastronomic delight.

Certainly this is not the sort of dessert you would have every day, it has far too many eggs, far too much cream and certainly too much white sugar. But it is a dessert that has a complex creamy elegance, and it is an ice-cream lover's dream.

Ice Cream

375 g (¾ lb) sugar
½ cup water
6 egg whites
pinch cream of tartar
900 ml (1 ½ pints) cream
1 tablespoon instant coffee, dissolved in an equal amount of hot water
2 tablespoons praline

Place the water and sugar in a pot and bring gently to the boil, making sure the sugar has dissolved before the liquid boils. Leave it to boil for 6 minutes. In the meantime put the egg whites in a large heat-resistant bowl and beat with the cream of tartar until the whites are firm but not dry. When the syrup has been boiling for 6 minutes, remove it from the heat and slowly pour it into the egg whites, beating as you pour. The whites will increase in volume and the sugar will cook them to a wonderful gloss. This is what is often referred to as 'Italian meringue'. Chill this mixture by sitting it in your freezer for half an hour.

Whip the cream, add the coffee and fold in the praline. Whip this to the same consistency as the Italian meringue, fold the two mixtures together and place in a container and freeze. You now have cappuccino ice cream.

Walnut *Brûlée*

6 egg yolks
½ cup sugar
1 cup cream
2 cups milk
vanilla seeds from ¼ vanilla bean (or 1 teaspoon vanilla extract)
3 tablespoons blanched, skinned and coarsely diced walnuts
brown sugar for caramelising
coffee powder for decoration

Preheat the oven to 120°C/250°F. Combine all the ingredients except the walnuts in a double-boiler and mix thoroughly but do not froth up. Cook on low heat until all the sugar has dissolved. Add the walnuts and pour into a baking dish. Place the dish in a large roasting pan and pour hot water around the dish, two-thirds of the way up the side. This creates a water bath, or bain-marie, that will gently cook the custard and stop it from catching. Bake for 20 minutes, and remember that eggs continue to cook once removed from the heat, so remove the brûlée from the oven a little before it is completely set. Chill the brûlée and when cold dust the top generously with brown sugar and grill until bubbling. Chill until needed.

To serve, take spoonfuls of the ice cream and put them quenelle style onto a large plate, place a spoonful of the brûlée to one side and dust with a little powdered coffee.

Notes

For walnut pralines, heat two cups of sugar over a medium heat and gently dissolve the sugar, cooking it until it colours. Place clusters of fresh, lightly toasted walnuts on a stainless steel bench or a roasting tray. As the sugar colours, gently pour the syrup over each cluster. It will set and stores well in an airtight container, hidden from late-night raiders and all those poor souls on a diet who need a sugar fix.

Hazelnuts make the most wonderful pralines. I would serve hazelnut pralines with a hazelnut brûlée, cappuccino ice cream and a drizzle of rum.

To achieve an evenly caramelised top on the brûlée, a very hot grill is needed. In professional kitchens we use a fiercely hot salamander. Many chefs use a blow-torch.

Brûlées can be made individually or in a large dish. Alter the cooking time to suit, as in a large dish it will take longer to get the middle of the brûlée completely cooked. If in doubt, I cook on a lower temperature than suggested and cook for longer. Whichever size you are cooking make sure that you adjust the heat so the water does not go above a gentle simmer. If the water boils the custard can curdle.

Brandied apricot brûlées with white chocolate are one of my favourites. On the base of a ramekin you sit a brandied apricot, into the custard you grate the white chocolate, and simply continue as per the recipe. A brûlée made with a dash of Sauternes and fresh berries is also a superb combination. Once mastered, the brûlée is a recipe that is as broad as your imagination.

Butterscotch Sauce

This sauce is great over plain ice cream with ginger brûlée, using crystallised ginger combined with a little ground ginger to give the brûlée some heat.

Method

Simmer the first 4 ingredients for about 4 minutes. Thicken with a little arrowroot or cornflour slackened in a small amount of water. Add cream if you wish to enrich the sauce. I wouldn't add cream here as both components of the dessert are quite rich enough as it is; however, this sauce is excellent with a Sunday tea of banana crêpes, and I would consider adding it then.

½ cup golden syrup
125 g (4 oz) brown sugar
½ cup water
30 g (1 oz) butter
arrowroot or cornflour to thicken
cream to enrich if you feel so inclined

Sherried Fruit Sauce

Of all dessert sauces, this is one of my favourites. The flavour is well balanced and yet with the addition of sherry and citric acid it is very hard to pick what is in the recipe. It makes a great dish with fresh fruit and warm crêpes, while a simple dish of banana, button meringues and fresh pineapple tossed with this sauce creates the ultimate in the nursery food that we all pretend not to love. The sauce base holds well in the fridge.

The piquant flavour of the steeped oranges and the subtle kick of this fruit sauce, when combined with small squares of puff pastry, create an elegant dessert sandwich. Cut 7 cm (3 in) squares of puff pastry, dust generously with icing sugar and bake until golden. Split the pastry and layer it with the drained oranges, dribble with the sauce and serve dusted again with icing sugar. It is very simple, yet for colour, texture and flavour it is a perfect combination.

Method

Cook the egg yolks, sugar, juices and citric acid in a double-boiler. Sprinkle in the gelatine and stir until a custard has formed, about 20 minutes over low heat. Cool slightly and add the sherry. The sauce can be stored in a covered container in the refrigerator at this stage. To serve, fold in an equal amount of lightly whipped cream, creating a superb sauce that goes with many flavours.

On its own the sauce goes very well with fresh fruit. Let guests help themselves to a bowl of this cream, and just make sure you have plenty. It's rich but very moreish.

4 egg yolks
¾ cup sugar
1 cup orange juice
½ cup pineapple juice
1 teaspoon citric acid
1 teaspoon gelatine
4 tablespoons dry sherry
whipped cream

'I *worry* just as any cook *does*, checking plates that come back after *guests* have finished their dinner, *asking* dining-room staff a *thousand times* "did everyone like it?", staying *awake* into the small hours trying to *improve* a dish *that* I am not totally *happy* with.'

confections with Coffee

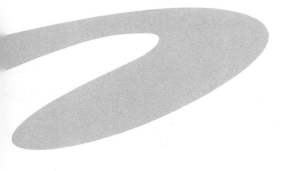

Basbousa	*165*
Caramelised Brie with Pickled Figs	*166*
Ricotta Pancakes with Sautéed Spiced Pears	*168*
Hot Almond Chocolate 'To Die For'	*169*
Stilton Shortbread	*169*
Chocolate Pots	*170*
Coconut Sour Cream Biscuits	*171*
Turkish Delight	*172*
Caramelised Walnuts with Citrus Marzipan	*173*
Ginger Chocolate Wontons with Orange Liqueur Sauce	*174*
White Chocolate Fudge with Hazelnut Praline	*176*
Potted Hazelnut Cheese with Avocado and Grapefruit Salad	*177*

*T**here* is nothing nicer than to sit down with a good cup of coffee, relax and enjoy the moment, whether it is at the end of a special dinner, after an evening at the opera, a night on the town, or simply a late supper with friends. I love late evening, a time to relax and enjoy a glass of Cognac, the company of good friends — and something delectable to accompany coffee.

It is here that we can orchestrate a surprise for special friends, perhaps pottles of hazelnut cheese accompanied by an avocado and grapefruit salad, mini toasts with well-flavoured rarebit, a caramelised brie with pickled fruits, or simply white chocolate shortbread with hot chocolate. It's a time to serve something truly special with coffee, something no one would expect, and to give our guests that little extra pampering.

Basbousa

200 g (6 oz) butter
250 g (8 oz) sugar
2½ cups semolina
1½ teaspoons baking powder
1 tablespoon vanilla extract
¾ cup yoghurt
½ cup whole almonds, blanched

I will always remember the first time I tasted basbousa. A group of friends and I had been to Carols by Candlelight, a tradition in Christchurch where thousands gather down by the banks of the River Avon on Christmas Eve. With candles and hymn sheets we sing our hearts out. This particular Christmas Eve, the evening was balmy, the singing was almost operatic, or so we thought, and the group of friends I was with all seemed to sparkle. It was a wonderful feeling, and afterwards we all went back to fellow-foodie Donald's city apartment, drank Margueritas for several hours, and then Donald brought out large trays of basbousa with strong black coffee. The flavour of the basbousa just seemed to complement the entire evening. Close friends on Christmas Eve sitting on the living-room floor discussing Christmases past and all the little things that make Christmas truly enjoyable for us, enjoying each other's company and simply savouring the moment. Basbousa was the 'icing on the cake'.

Method

Preheat the oven to 180°C/350°F. Melt the butter and combine it with all the other ingredients except the almonds. Pour into a well-buttered sponge-roll tin. Mark into small diamonds, pressing an almond into each. Bake for about 20 minutes, or until just beginning to colour. Mark the diamonds again and pour the syrup over the basbousa while still hot. As the basbousa cools it will absorb all the syrup so do not worry if it looks as if you are drowning the cooked mixture.

Syrup

¾ cup water
2 cups sugar
5 tablespoons lemon juice
2 teaspoons citric acid

Combine all the ingredients in a medium-sized pot and bring to a simmer. As soon as the sugar is dissolved remove from the heat and keep hot.

Notes

Once cooled, basbousa is best removed from the sponge tin and stored in an airtight container. The citric acid and lemon juice often react with the tin and can cause the base to discolour.

Basbousa will freeze well, and should be thawed in the fridge gently overnight. It is excellent served as a dessert with lightly whipped cream and perhaps some delicious gilded almonds for decoration.

The oranges steeped in green ginger go very well with the basbousa and make another excellent dessert, without the crêpe.

Caramelised Brie *with* Pickled Figs

1 whole brie, firm but ripe
2 cups sugar
¼ cup water
3 cups various toasted nuts (e.g. walnuts, pecans, cashews, hazelnuts, macadamias, almonds or pistachios)
½ cup crystallised ginger
grated zest of 2 lemons

Method

Combine the sugar and water in a medium-sized pan and bring to the boil, cooking gently until it is a deep golden colour. Brush down the sides of the saucepan with a small brush dipped in cold water if the sugar begins to form crystals on the side of the pot.

While the sugar is boiling combine the nuts with the ginger and lemon zest and spread evenly across the top of the brie. When the sugar has reached a good caramel colour slowly pour it over the brie. The caramel will set firmly, adhering the nuts to the top, and it will be quite difficult to serve, but glorious to taste.

Once the caramel has set and cooled, place the brie on a large platter with a selection of crackers, croûtons and pickled figs. I also like to serve crisp chilled pear. The guests crack the toffee with the back of a spoon and scoop out some of the brie with the toffee and nuts. Small side plates are a good idea.

Pickled Figs

3 kg (6 lb) dried figs
cloves
1 cup water
1 l (1¾ pints) white wine vinegar
1½ kg (3 lb) sugar
1 tablespoon mixed spices
extra 500 g (1 lb) sugar

Push 1 clove into each fig. Boil the water, vinegar, sugar and spices for 15 minutes then add the figs. Boil slowly for an hour. Water may need to be added if the figs are too dry and sucking up the liquid fast. Once boiled, allow to stand overnight.

The next day bring to the boil, drain the figs and place them in hot, clean bottles. Add 500 g (1 lb) of sugar to the syrup and bring it to the boil; boil for 30 minutes, pour over the figs and seal.

Notes

When caught short and wishing to serve a whole brie, I often use sun-dried tomato pesto, bought locally. Slicing the top off the brie, I cut it into wedges but leave them in the whole shape. With a spoon I carefully push a few tablespoons of pesto down between each wedge so it is flush with the top of the brie, tie a piece of cooking string around the rim to hold it, and slide it into a preheated oven for 10-15 minutes. When it comes out, starting to melt on the top, I pat on some pre-toasted pinenuts and decorate it with a garland of fresh basil leaves. It is very simple to make and tastes superb; best with crisp crackers or French bread croûtons.

Black grapes are a wonderful alternative to pickled figs.

CONFECTIONS WITH COFFEE

167

Ricotta Pancakes *with* Sautéed Spiced Pears

I particularly love this recipe on a cold frosty evening, when the fires are all lit and it looks as though the evening guests may have to stay the night — an occurrence that often happens in Christchurch when the frost could set oil in the pantry. These fluffy pancakes are easy to put together and perfect eaten straight away, although they can be prepared up to a day ahead, refrigerated and heated gently to serve.

Pear *Topping*

Peel, core and dice the pears into 2 cm (1 in) dice. Melt the butter in a large frying pan over medium-high heat. Add the pears and sauté for about 5 minutes, or until the pears are softened. Add the sugar and continue cooking until the sauce is slightly caramelised, about 3 minutes. Add the ginger, cinnamon, orange juice and vanilla and cook for another minute. Cover and set aside.

Pancakes

For the pancakes, combine the egg yolks, ricotta, sugar, orange zest and flour in a medium-sized mixing bowl and whisk until well combined.

Beat the egg whites in a separate bowl with the pinch of salt until stiff but not dry. Fold the whites gently into the pancake mixture and cook the pancakes in a frypan that has been heated with about 1 tablespoon of butter. Cook the pancakes for 2–3 minutes on each side and serve immediately with a large dollop of pear topping. Simply heaven on a cold night with mugs of hot chocolate.

Do not worry if your first few pancakes dissolve in a mess when you go to turn them over. Turn up the heat and cook the next batch longer before you are tempted to turn them over.

---

3 large ripe pears (Anjou are perfect)
2 tablespoons butter
3 tablespoons sugar
generous pinch of ground ginger
generous pinch of ground cinnamon
1 tablespoon fresh orange juice
1 teaspoon vanilla extract

4 large eggs, separated
1 cup ricotta cheese
2 tablespoons sugar
zest from 1 orange
½ cup flour
pinch of salt
butter to fry

Hot Almond Chocolate *'To Die For'*

This is my favourite hot chocolate drink that does not have alcohol in it. I make this with white chocolate of course, but use your favourite — white, dark or milk — and alter the mixture to suit your taste. A dash of brandy is great, but not necessary, and I only add it when I am feeling sorry for myself, or simply wish to have a special treat. We make this drink at Michaels in winter, serving it as an alternative to coffee at the end of the evening. This recipe makes enough for two people, as surely you would not drink something so sublime on your own?

60 g (2 oz) chocolate
2 tablespoons honey
1 tablespoon ground almonds
1 teaspoon good vanilla extract
2 cups hot milk

Method

Melt the chocolate and honey in a small double-boiler and add the almonds and vanilla. Whisk the milk and pour it into the chocolate base. Serve in hot mugs.

Stilton Shortbread

Just to keep my restless nature satisfied, here is a product with as many permutations as there are original recipes for Caesar salad. I have tried them all, from white chocolate shortbread to black pepper, from Scottish to fresh tarragon and orange, from truffled with dried mushroom to one enriched with fresh parmigiano reggiano. This Stilton shortbread is one I enjoy serving and it has become a favourite of many of my family.

60 g (2 oz) butter
90 g (3 oz) Stilton
1 cup flour, sifted
1 tablespoon rice flour
cayenne to taste

Method

Preheat the oven to 180°C/350°F. Beat the butter and Stilton together until soft and creamy. Beat in the flours and cayenne and knead together, shaping into a 15 cm (6 in) roll. Wrap in plastic wrap and refrigerate for 2 hours.

Cut the roll into 24 slices, place on a baking sheet, and bake for 15 minutes, until cooked. Sprinkle each shortbread with cayenne and store in airtight containers.

Chocolate Pots

My mother, who is a great lover of both chocolate and caramel, and the person who introduced me to good walnuts, not simply walnuts, gave me the components of this recipe. It is truly the epitome of her cooking. This dark chocolate puts me in such a bad mood and gives me such a ripping headache that I daren't eat it for the safety of my staff. It is, however, such a brilliant and much-loved recipe that we should not delete it for that reason. The majestic combination is of good old caramel sauce, lightly roasted walnuts and a brandied chocolate ganache. The subsequent dish is one of individual chocolates set in little eggcups with their proud domes, firm exteriors and melting, moist caramel interiors with the crunch of walnut.

The most divine accompaniment to coffee, whether it is after dinner, late after a show, or simply to give you a little energy kick at afternoon tea time.

Caramel

Combine all the ingredients in a double-boiler and heat gently for about 20 minutes, until the sugar has dissolved and the caramel has coloured. This can be done well in advance and the mixture stored in an airtight container.

1 tin sweetened condensed milk
125 g (4 oz) butter
3 tablespoons golden syrup
¾ cup sugar

Chocolate *Ganache*

Heat the chocolate, cream and brandy gently in a double-boiler, taking care not to get any water in with the chocolate. It will take about 10 minutes for the chocolate to melt and combine with the cream and brandy. Stir gently and put to one side.

In china eggcups, small ramekins or espresso coffee cups, put ½ teaspoon of walnuts, top this with 2 teaspoons of caramel and top with the chocolate. Leave this to set; when firm, drizzle a little more chocolate on top to give a dome effect.

These can be plastic wrapped and stored in the fridge but need to be removed half an hour before serving to come back to room temperature.

Serve on a small plate with a teaspoon as an accompaniment to coffee, on a dessert plate with a dollop of cream and fresh fruit as a small taste treat after the opera, or accompany with ginger ice cream and serve with a good dry sherry as a wonderful small dessert course.

200 g (6 oz) dark cooking chocolate, grated
¼ cup cream
¼ cup brandy
¼ cup roasted and lightly chopped walnuts

Coconut Sour Cream Biscuits

I do not profess to be a good baker, in fact I do not profess to be able to bake much at all, but this recipe even I cannot get wrong. It's all done in one bowl, is a synch to put together, and stores so well that there is no excuse not to have something to sweeten the tooth. It is excellent as an accompaniment to ice cream, sorbet or a fresh fruit sabayon, delicious with coffee or our almond hot chocolate, with Irish coffee on a cold night, or chilled lemon tea in the height of summer.

2 eggs
3 egg yolks
300 g (10 oz) sugar
3 tablespoons sour cream
300 g (10 oz) desiccated coconut

Method

Beat the eggs and egg yolks with the sugar until they are light and fluffy. Stir in the sour cream and coconut. Place small teaspoons on a buttered tray and bake at 180°C/350°F for 10 minutes, or until lightly browned. Allow to cool and store in airtight containers or in the freezer.

'I do not *profess* to be a good *baker*, in *fact* I do not profess *to be* able to bake much at *all*.'

Turkish Delight

This Turkish delight is one of the recipes I inherited from the wonderful Sophia Magdalene when I purchased the restaurant. A talented cook, painter and educationalist, she could blow your tiny brains with her knowledge, and I must say her courage and style helped me a lot through the first few years of owning a restaurant.

Out the window shot my social life, my health and my much-loved savings, and in came heartache, extreme tiredness, and I blossomed into a barrel of lard in no time. It was hell and there are no two ways about it, but for some absurd reason it was inspiring at the same time. It was a little like university, with that feeling of whatever you do, however hard you work, there is still more work to do; you just might have been able to do it better with more hours in the day, and you feel guilty when you don't show results. The food business is not 'just a piece of cake', but every so often out of it all comes a recipe like this to make it all worthwhile.

Notes

I sieve my icing sugar and cornflour and toss the Turkish delight through this, gently tossing it in the sieve again to let all the spare powder fall through. This way you get a good even coating of powder.

Toasted walnuts are delightful in Turkish delight. The best way to incorporate them is to spread the walnuts on the base of the sponge-roll tin before you pour in the syrup. Leave to set, and slice.

Peppermint essence and a dash of green colouring gives you an exquisite variation. Or add the zest and juice of three lemons and a drop of yellow food colouring for a refreshing Turkish delight. Toasted almonds and orange juice will give you a wonderful flavour as well, and perhaps add some zest of the orange to the icing sugar and cornflour mix to give that extra kick.

Method

Combine the sugar, gelatine, cream of tartar and water in a medium-sized pot and bring to the boil gently, stirring regularly with a wooden spoon. Boil until the liquid sheets when you lift out the spoon. By sheeting I mean the syrup will fall from the spoon in a broad, almost jelly like, sheet. Add the rosewater and red food colouring, pour into a buttered sponge-roll tin and leave to set. Do not put it in the refrigerator.

Combine the cornflour and icing sugar and when the Turkish delight has set cut it into small squares and toss it in the icing-sugar mix. Store in airtight containers with wax paper between each layer. Turkish delight will store for up to 3 weeks airtight, but may need to be dusted again with icing sugar mix to refresh it.

4½ cups sugar
4½ tablespoons gelatine
2 teaspoons cream of tartar
2½ cups water
2 teaspoons rosewater
small dash red food colouring
2 tablespoons cornflour
4 tablespoons icing sugar

Caramelised Walnuts *with* Citrus Marzipan

My youngest niece and nephew, Amelia and William, just love to make these. I make up the caramel and have it just warm enough to dip, keeping the pot in a bath of warm water. It is surprising how when we have finished we often have no more than five caramelised walnuts left.

At Christmas we tie small gold ribbons around each walnut, and when dipped in toffee and firm, they make magnificent Christmas tree decorations. Edible gold leaf laid on top at the last moment of setting can give the tree a wonderful glitter, but I am sure would be best not eaten by the children. On Boxing Day when we have 'the family picnic' these are devoured by adults and children alike, along with any other edible Christmas decorations we may have made: little Christmas trees made from white chocolate shortbread and tied up with a tartan bow; wonton parcels filled with whisky-soaked Christmas mince, baked, chilled, dipped in white chocolate and tied up with a gold thread; almond cookies baked in the shape of a star, dusted with edible silver and studded with silver almonds; tiny Christmas crackers made from sour-cream pastry and rolled to enclose Cognac-soaked crystallised fruits; and, most importantly, little balls of white chocolate fudge rolled in hazelnut praline and tied up with ribbons.

Method

90 g (3 oz) marzipan
fine zest of 1 lemon
fine zest of 1 orange
40 walnut halves
200 g (6 oz) sugar
125 ml (4 fl oz) water

Mix the marzipan and zests together and sandwich the walnut halves with a marble-sized amount.

In a heavy-based saucepan, combine the sugar and water and bring to the boil over a gentle heat. Cook until it is a rich caramel colour, about 10 minutes, and if crystals form on the side of the pot, brush them down with a wet pastry brush. Take care not to get burnt. With a pair of tongs, dip the marzipan-filled walnuts very lightly into the caramel, shake off any excess, and sit them on a lightly oiled baking tray. The trick with this recipe is to have just a thin coating of caramel, not something that is so thick it gives you lockjaw when you go to eat it.

Ginger Chocolate Wontons *with* Orange Liqueur Sauce

Wontons are often overlooked, especially as part of a sweet course. These little wonders are superb in that they can be made up, frozen and cooked direct from the freezer as required. Perfect for unexpected guests, or for the end of a formal dinner party, presented on large silver trays, dusted with icing sugar and with a jug of sauce to one side, as a little surprise for an after-show supper or to go with coffee on a cool autumn day.

Make them when you are in the mood for working with chocolate and freeze them in large airtight containers for later when you know you will be busy. Add brandy and Christmas mince to the filling and use them as little sweetmeats for entertaining, add white chocolate instead of dark, use dried apricot and some orange and give them a little kick with Kirsch. Use your imagination and what is in the cupboard and come up with your own combination. A chocoholic can always think of other ways of using chocolate.

CONFECTIONS WITH COFFEE

60 g (2 oz) cream cheese
125 g (4 oz) chocolate, grated
60 g (2 oz) crystallised ginger, finely chopped
60 g (2 oz) slivered almonds, lightly toasted
2 tablespoons fine cake or breadcrumbs
grated zest and juice of 1 orange
1 packet wonton wrappers
oil to deep-fry
icing sugar to dust

Method

In a sauté pan gently heat the cream cheese to soften, then add the chocolate, ginger, almonds, cake crumbs, zest and juice of the orange. Mix well with a wooden spoon, heating until all are combined and no flecks of cream cheese show. Don't let the mixture cool as it will firm up too much and become difficult to work with.

Lay out the wonton wrappers, and put a teaspoon of chocolate filling in the centre of each wrapper. Brush the edges of the wrapper with water and pull the sides up, pouch fashion. Place on a lightly oiled tray and chill. Do not sit them on a tray dusted with cornflour as this will very quickly ruin the deep-fry oil.

Heat the oil to 180°C/350°F, then drop in a few chocolate parcels at a time. Lift them out as soon as they are coloured and put them to one side. If the chocolate is coming out you are either cooking them for too long, the wontons are not chilled enough, or you have not pulled the edges in enough to seal the filling. Cooking the wontons from frozen is often best as the wrapper will cook to crisp, the chocolate will warm and begin to melt but the filling will not come rushing out.

Orange *Liqueur* Sauce

Melt the butter in a small pot over a low heat. In the bowl of a beater combine the egg yolks and sugar, and beat until light and fluffy. Add the melted butter, beating until well combined. Place the mixture in a saucepan, add the liqueur and cream, and whisk over a low heat until thickened. Do not allow it to boil. Cool. Blanch the orange zest to remove the bitterness and add to the sauce just before serving.

60 g (2 oz) unsalted butter
3 egg yolks
½ cup castor sugar
2 tablespoons Grand Marnier
¼ cup cream
zest from 1 orange

'I am a *night* person. I *adore* the *buzz* of a busy *kitchen* and the sounds *and* smells of a *happy* dining *room*.'

White Chocolate Fudge *with* Hazelnut Praline

Rolled small, these are great as sweetmeats after a formal dinner, as a sweet with coffee, or as something special to take to a picnic.

The white chocolate fudge is excellent dropped into hot milk and whisked for a winter toddy with a splash of rum. What could be better than to be tucked up in your Peter Rabbit pyjamas, with a good cookbook, Beethoven's *Pastoral Symphony* playing quietly in the background, a roaring fire and a white chocolate toddy, the ultimate nursery drink for grown-ups.

Praline

125 g (4 oz) sugar
125 g (4 oz) hazelnuts

Combine the sugar and hazelnuts in a pot and heat over a low heat, slowly melting the sugar and lightly cooking the hazelnuts. Turn the heat up and stir with a wooden spoon. The sugar will stick to the spoon, but continue to stir and it will dissolve. When the mixture is golden pour it onto an oiled stainless-steel bench or oiled oven tray. Let it cool then grind to a powder in a blender or kitchen processor. Store in an airtight jar.

Fudge

90 g (3 oz) crystallised papaya, finely chopped
90 g (3 oz) crystallised pineapple, finely chopped
90 g (3 oz) crystallised ginger, finely chopped
1 400 g (13 oz) tin sweetened condensed milk
500 g (1 lb) white chocolate, grated (dark cooking chocolate also makes great fudge)
½ teaspoon vanilla essence
praline powder

Soak the finely chopped papaya, pineapple and ginger in just enough boiling water to cover. Let them sit for an hour, then drain and dry the fruit.

Butter and paper-line a sponge-roll tin.

Into a pot put the condensed milk, grated chocolate and crystallised fruit. Gently melt over low heat, stirring frequently until the mixture has combined well and the chocolate has melted. Add the vanilla. Pour into the prepared tin and leave to set. Once set, roll the fudge into balls using a melon baller, an ice-cream scoop or a small spoon, and roll in the ground praline. Leave to rest, preferably overnight.

Notes

These freeze well, and in fact when frozen are perfect to drop into warm melted dark chocolate. Leave them to drain on a cake rack. The look of white and dark chocolate is always luxurious.

I have this fudge made up and keep it in the freezer. It's all part of my weight-loss programme! However, when I make it to freeze I omit the crystallised fruits but add praline to the fudge itself. This is cut into small squares and is just perfect straight from the freezer into the hot milk for one of my toddies. It is just right to box up and give as a gift, and looks good on an after-theatre platter or as something smart to give guests, more often than not guests I have forgotten I've invited.

Potted Hazelnut Cheese *with* Avocado *and* Grapefruit Salad

Method

pinch of saffron threads
1 tablespoon hot water
60 g (2 oz) butter
300 ml (½ pint) cream
150 g (5 oz) roasted and ground hazelnuts
¼ teaspoon cayenne
4 egg yolks
500 g (1 lb) grated tasty cheese
salt and freshly ground white pepper

Put the saffron threads into the water and leave to steep for 10 minutes. Put all the ingredients, including the saffron and water, into a double-boiler and heat gently for 15 minutes. Stir until the mixture is well combined and the cheese has melted. Check seasoning and pour into medium-sized ramekins or small crocks, teacups or little terracotta pots. Leave to set and serve with the following salad.

Avocado and Grapefruit *Salad*

2 avocados
2 grapefruit
4 tablespoons finely chopped onion
6 teaspoons dry English mustard
1 cup honey
1 cup lemon juice
1 teaspoon salt
1¼ cups olive oil

Peel and stone the avocados; peel the grapefruit, taking care to remove all pith, then segment. Combine the onion, mustard, honey, lemon juice and salt in a blender and slowly drizzle in the oil with the machine running. Toss the avocado and grapefruit in a small amount of this dressing and pile it onto 4 large dinner plates. Serve the hazelnut cheese to one side and a few salad greens as decoration. A delicious dish to serve late when everyone is hungry but sweet food is not suitable, and just exquisite with a light white wine that has a high acidity level to cope with the dressing.

back to basics

Crêpes	181
Tartlet Base	181
Cream Cheese Pastry	181
Mayonnaise	182
Hollandaise	182
Sweet French Dressing	182
Crème Fraîche	182
Light Homemade Mayonnaise	183
Herb Mayonnaise	183
Beef Stock	183
Basic Chicken Stock	184
Mushroom Stock	184
Light Fish Stock	185
Wine and Vegetable Stock	185

MICHAEL LEE-RICHARDS ❧ COOK!

'In *cooking*, the *basics* *are* the *most* important things.'

Crêpes

3 cups flour
2 cups milk
1½ cups water
5 eggs
1 teaspoon salt
⅓ cup oil

Put all in a blender and whizz at high speed. If possible, leave to stand for 1–2 hours.

For yellow crêpes add 2 teaspoons turmeric; for green crêpes use spinach purée.

Heat a crêpe pan and lightly oil it. Swirl around just enough of the crêpe mixture to coat the pan and pour out the excess. Turn when cooked on one side. When the crêpes are all cooked, pack them in foil with freezer paper between each, and freeze until needed.

Makes approximately 40.

Tartlet *Base*

Place the flour, salt and butter in a food processor, and process for about 10 seconds, until the mixture resembles coarse meal. Add water a drop at a time until the dough holds together. Wrap and chill for at least an hour. The dough can be frozen at this stage.

Roll out the dough and cut it to fit your tins. Chill well. Preheat the oven to 150°C/300°F. Weight each mould with paper and rice and bake until lightly coloured. Remove weights and re-crisp in the oven. Chill on a rack and store airtight until needed. Freezes well.

Makes 40.

2½ cups flour
1 teaspoon salt
250 g (½ lb) butter, cut into small pieces
¼–½ cup ice water

Cream Cheese Pastry

250 g (8 oz) soft butter (at room temperature)
250 g (8 oz) cream cheese (at room temperature)
2 cups flour
2 tablespoons sugar

This makes a very simple, rough puff-style pastry that is excellent for pies, tarts etc. Beat all in a whizz. Chill for 1 hour before use.

Makes 1 kg.

Mayonnaise

2 egg yolks
½ teaspoon dry English mustard powder
few drops fresh lemon juice
½ teaspoon salt
1 tablespoon white wine vinegar
few drops tabasco
300 ml (½ pint) best olive oil

Place in a blender the egg yolks, mustard, lemon juice, salt, vinegar, and a few drops of tabasco, along with 4 tablespoons of oil. Start the machine and slowly dribble in the rest of the oil until a thick, creamy emulsion is created. More or less oil may be needed depending on the speed at which it is poured and the quality of the oil.

Aïoli is mayonnaise richly flavoured with garlic. For apple aïoli, add grated apple. Makes 375 ml.

Hollandaise

Heat the butter in a small sauté pan until it is boiling. Place the egg yolks, lemon juice and tabasco in a blender or kitchen whizz and blend. While still blending, slowly pour in the butter. This will cook the eggs and create a wonderful creamy hollandaise. Check seasoning and store. Freezes well.

Makes approximately 300 ml.

250 g (8 oz) butter
6 egg yolks
1 tablespoon lemon juice
2 drops tabasco
salt and pepper to season

Sweet *French* Dressing

2½ cups vinegar
4 cups oil
6 heaped tablespoons sugar
1 teaspoon salt
2 teaspoons white pepper
2 whole garlic cloves, peeled
2 tablespoons Dijon mustard
1 medium-sized onion
1 tablespoon lemon juice
generous pinch of parsley
1 teaspoon peppercorns

Combine all in a blender and mix well. Stores well.
Makes 6 cups.

Crème Fraîche

Heat the cream over low heat to exactly 110°C/225°F. Add the sour cream and mix well. Put in a covered jar and let sit at room temperature for 6–8 hours. Refrigerate for at least 24 hours before serving. The crème fraîche will become thick like sour cream. It can be kept refrigerated in a tightly covered jar for 2–3 weeks.

Makes 2 cups.

2 cups cream
2 tablespoons sour cream

BACK TO BASICS

Light *Homemade* Mayonnaise

2 eggs
¼ teaspoon dry mustard
¾ teaspoon salt
2 tablespoons freshly squeezed lemon juice
½ cup olive oil
1½ cups vegetable or safflower oil
salt to taste

Mix the eggs, mustard, salt and lemon juice in the bowl of a food processor. With the motor on, add the oil, drop by drop, until the mixture begins to thicken. Add the remaining oil in a steady stream and process until smooth. Season to taste (you may also want to add more lemon juice) and refrigerate.

Makes approximately 2½ cups.

Herb Mayonnaise

250 g (8 oz) fresh spinach leaves, washed and dried
2 tablespoons chopped shallots
¼ cup loosely packed watercress leaves (no stems)
¼ cup chopped fresh parsley
2 tablespoons coarsely chopped fresh tarragon leaves

Bring a small pot of water to the boil, add the spinach, shallots, watercress, parsley and tarragon, and boil for 1 minute. Drain and immediately rinse with cold water to stop the cooking. Drain again and pat dry with a towel. Finely chop by hand or in a food processor. It may then be stirred into the Light Homemade Mayonnaise.

Makes approximately 2½ cups.

Beef *Stock*

2 large onions with skins, each cut into eighths
1 leek, trimmed, washed, and cut into 3 pieces
½ head garlic, unpeeled, cut in half crosswise
3–4 stalks celery with tops, washed and cut into pieces
1–2 small carrots, unpeeled and each cut into 4 pieces
1 kg (2 lb) beef bones (preferably marrow and knuckle bones)
1 kg (2 lb) veal bones (preferably shin, knuckle, and feet, or a combination)
1 large oxtail, cut into small pieces, or several small oxtails
water (just to cover)
4 whole cloves
1 bayleaf
1 bunch fresh thyme
10 black peppercorns
2–3 fresh hot peppers, jalapeno or arbol, or 1–2 dried red hot chilli peppers (optional)

Preheat the oven to 190°C/375°F.

Place all the vegetables in a very large, deep roasting pan so that they cover the bottom of the pan. Arrange the bones over the vegetables and roast in the upper third of the oven for 1 hour.

Remove from oven and, with a slotted spoon, transfer all the bones and vegetables to a large stockpot. Pour off the fat from the roasting pan and deglaze the pan with 1 litre (2 pints) of water. Pour this into the stockpot. Add cloves, bayleaf, thyme, peppercorns, hot peppers and cover with water. Bring to a boil, skimming off the scum as it rises to the surface. Lower the heat, stir, cover, and simmer for 2 hours.

Remove the stock from the heat and let it cool undisturbed. Strain through a fine sieve or a strainer lined with a double thickness of cheesecloth. Discard the bones, vegetables and herbs, and let the stock rest for 15 minutes to allow the fat to rise to the surface. Degrease the stock and use immediately, refrigerate or freeze.

Basic *Chicken* Stock

Place chicken in a pot and cover with water. Add remaining ingredients and bring slowly to the boil. Simmer for 1½ hours, removing any scum that comes to the top and adding extra water if required. Strain and store the stock in the fridge until needed. It can also be frozen for later use.

Notes

The choice of vegetables is as important as the meat used. Onions must be of the ordinary yellow type. Go easy on the use of carrots; their sugar should be a hint and not a statement.

Thyme, bay and parsley (bouquet garni) should never be wrapped in cheesecloth; they should be able to float freely in the liquid to render their flavour.

Leek is the soul of the stock. But be careful, use the light-green part and approximately 4 cm (2 in) of the dark green. Keep the wonderful white part for garnish or a vegetable dish. Discard the rest of the dark green part.

White wine is acid and helps the bones to release a maximum of gelatine and flour.

2 kg (4 lb) chicken bones, washed in cold water
water to cover, 2 cm (1 in) above bones
½ cup each of coarsely chopped leek (or onion), carrot and celery
1 bayleaf
8 stalks parsley
½ tablespoon peppercorns
dash white wine (optional)

Mushroom Stock

Simmer for 20 minutes, then strain. Keep in the fridge until needed, or freeze.

1 l (2 pints) chicken or vegetable stock
1½ cups mushroom scraps and trimmings
1 onion, finely chopped
1 carrot, finely chopped
12 peppercorns
2 cloves garlic
4 parsley stalks
1 bayleaf
1 tablespoon Worcestershire sauce
salt and pepper

Light Fish Stock

500 g (1 lb) fish bones and heads
1 onion, finely diced
1 leek, washed and finely diced
1 carrot, peeled and finely diced
¼ celery stalk, finely diced
125 g (4 oz) firm white button mushrooms, washed and finely chopped
1 tablespoon butter
freshly ground white pepper
200 ml (8 fl oz) dry white wine
1 l (2 pints) cold water
a small bunch of parsley, wrapped in muslin

This light stock can be used for a variety of fish dishes where the flavour of the sauce needs to be heightened or intensified. It can be stored to use as required, but try to make the stock from the bones of the fish you are using in the recipe. This will give the finished dish a unified flavour.

Method

Cut off the fish gills with scissors. Roughly chop the bones and soak them in cold running water for 2–3 minutes. Drain and reserve.

Put all the prepared vegetables in a large pan with the butter, season with 8 turns of the pepper mill and sweat for 1–2 minutes without colouring. Add the fish bones and heads and sweat for a further minute. Pour in the wine, boil for a few seconds to remove the alcohol, then add 1 litre (2 pints) cold water and the parsley. Boil for not more than 1–2 minutes and skim. Simmer gently for about 15 minutes, then strain the stock through a fine conical sieve into a large bowl, pressing the bones lightly with a ladle. Leave to cool before storing.

The stock will keep in a covered container for 2–3 days in the fridge, or for several weeks in the freezer.

Notes

When you boil the wine, the stock will turn cloudy for a moment. This is perfectly normal; it will clear when you add the cold water.

Wine and Vegetable Stock

Combine all the ingredients in a pan. Bring to a boil and simmer gently with a lid partly ajar for about 20 minutes. Strain. Reduce if you wish to strengthen the flavour. This stock keeps well in the fridge for 48 hours, but is best frozen if you are keeping it longer.

2 cups dry white wine
3 cups water
1 small onion, finely diced
1 small leek, thinly sliced
1 small carrot, finely chopped
1 bayleaf
small strip lemon peel
5 peppercorns
pinch of salt
sprig of fresh thyme

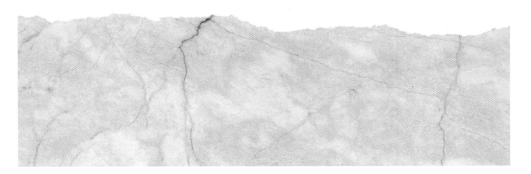

GLOSSARY

Aïoli ❧ Mayonnaise richly flavoured with garlic. It is excellent with vegetables, fish and grilled steak. Add grated apple for apple aïoli, finely chopped herbs for a tasty green aïoli, and roasted red peppers and black olives for a richly flavoured aïoli that is excellent with cold chicken.

Bain-marie ❧ A water bath, used for cooking and for keeping food warm. A bowl or saucepan is placed in a large container which is then filled with hot water.

Beurre manie ❧ Equal quantities of flour and softened butter worked to a paste and added as a liaison to thicken soups, sauces and stews.

Burghul wheat ❧ Also called bulgar or cracked wheat. This is a coarse cracked wheat that has been cooked and dried and always needs to be reconstituted. Excellent for salads.

Citron ❧ A variety of lemon that originated in the Himalayan region. Its main use today is in the form of candied peel. Can be used as a substitute for Seville oranges.

Clarify ❧ To clear stock by straining through cooked egg whites, or to make butter clear by heating, separating and discarding milk solids.

Coriander ❧ Also known as cilantro or Chinese parsley, this is an earthy-flavoured, aromatic herb which makes a good addition to salad. It is superb with fish and is frequently used in Thai cooking.

Coulis ❧ An unthickened purée, frequently made of fresh fruit or vegetable and used as a sauce, for example red pepper coulis or raspberry coulis.

Couscous ❧ A fine semolina made from wheat grain. More often than not it will have been precooked and merely needs to be moistened and steamed to heat through.

Crème Frâiche ❧ This cream is slightly acidic in taste, making it particularly good in sauces.

Demi-glace ❧ This is made by heavily reducing a well-made stock to a syrupy consistency for later use in cooking.

Duxelles ❧ A finely chopped mixture of sautéed mushrooms, shallots and herbs. It is often used as stuffing.

Escalope ❧ A term used for a cut, slice or scoop of meat or fish without any bones, gristle or skin. It is often flattened out and fried in butter.

Fish sauce ❧ Also called nam pla, this is a salty brown sauce similar to soy sauce and made from fish extract and salt.

Hoisan sauce ❧ A thick soybean-based sweet Chinese sauce usually mixed with other condiments for marinades and sauces.

GLOSSARY

Julienne A term that refers to the cutting of vegetables, meats, etc into matchstick size.

Ketchup manis A thick dark sauce that tastes very much like soy sauce and molasses combined. Excellent for enriching sauces and beef dishes, it is frequently used in Eastern cuisine.

Mascarpone A rich Italian cream cheese that has a very high fat content. The flavour is quite sweet, making it excellent for use in desserts but also good in savoury dishes.

Nori Edible seaweed. It is a greenish-black colour and is sold in thin sheets. Excellent for garnish or wrapped around rice rolls, it is perfect for finger food creations.

Polenta Also called cornmeal or maize meal. This is a yellow ground maize that is frequently used in Italian and American cuisine.

Prosciutto Salted, air-cured ham, sometimes known as Parma ham.

Quenelles An egg shape, more elegant than a ball. It can be achieved in soft, firm food by a long shallow scoop that is then rolled.

Raclette A splendid, well-flavoured Swiss cheese with a very high fat content that melts quickly. Strong-smelling, it goes well with both vegetables and meats.

Radicchio An Italian red-leafed lettuce that is quite bitter. There are many varieties; not all are red in colour.

Saffron The most expensive spice in the world. The fine red-yellow threads are the stamens of the saffron crocus. When added to a dish they release an unusual and delicious metallic flavour and a glorious yellow colour.

Shallot One of the mildest members of the onion family, the shallot is purplish-grey in colour and delicate in flavour. Look for firm bulbs. Shallots can be used in the same way as onions and are particularly suitable for pickling.

Spring onions Also called green onions and scallions.

Tabasco A proprietary brand of pepper sauce.

Tamarind A wonderful addition to sauces, meats and chutneys. This is a brittle brown seedpod that grows on trees. When the dried pod is peeled, soaked and strained it produces a thick paste with a unique flavour that is both sweet and tart.

Wasabi Green horseradish, often sold in either powder or paste form.

Zester A small utensil used specifically to remove the outer layer of citrus fruits. It is excellent with cucumbers and other firm vegetables or fruits.

INDEX

Akaroa Walnut Tart with Green Grape Glaze 144
Apple Clafoutis with Peppered Raclette and Crisp Mint Salad 112
Avocado and Sugar-Cured Bacon Wrapped in Yoghurt Pastry 74
Avocado Blini with Whitebait 24
Basbousa 165
Basic Chicken Stock 184
Bean Salsa 25
Beef Stock 183
Beef with Mustard and Cognac 122
Black Grape and Cardamom Sorbet 85
Bouillon of Autumn Mushrooms like a Cappucino 52
Braised Rabbit with Warm Lentil Salad 108
Buttered Noodles 119
Butterscotch Sauce 160
Canterbury Turnip and Blue Cheese Soup 54
Cappucino Ice Cream with Spooned Walnut Brûlée 158
Caramelised Brie with Pickled Figs 166
Caramelised Walnuts with Citrus Marzipan 173
Cathedral Salad of Herbs with Champagne Dressing and Witloof 96
Cauliflower and Orange Bisque 50
Chicken Almondine 28
Chicken with Plum and Walnuts 132
Chicken with Yoghurt and Red Pepper Coulis 134
Chilli Spiced Almonds with Cumin 36
Chocolate Pots 170
Coconut Cake with Warm Conserve 154
Coconut Sour Cream Biscuits 171
Coriander Tuiles with Pickled Grilled Scallops 78
Cream Cheese Pastry 181
Cream of Celery and Almond Soup 55
Crème Brûlée of Garlic with Smoked Salmon Croûtons 124
Crème Fraîche 182
Crêpes 181
Duck and Wild Rice Salad with Roasted Oranges 88
Duck Pie with Port and Grapefruit 120
Duck with Cardamom, Honey and Brandied Raisins 111
Fillet Steak with Old-Fashioned Stuffing, Green Peppercorns and Whisky 130
Galette of Leek with Fig Tapenade and Salad of Lamb Shoulder 76
Ginger Chocolate Wontons with Orange Liqueur Sauce 174
Grapefruit and Tequila Sorbet 86
Grilled Raddichio with Chilli Beef 40
Herb Mayonnaise 183
Herbed Rabbit Clafoutis with Fresh Grape Chutney 66
Hollandaise 182
Homemade Saffron Ricotta 39
Horseradish-Crusted Beef with Winter Pesto and Vinegar-Baked Potatoes 116
Hot Almond Chocolate 'To Die For' 169
Hot Salad of Beef with Basil 91
Lamb with Oranges and Anchovies 107
Lemon Syllabub Torte 142
Light Fish Stock 185
Light Homemade Mayonnaise 183
Little Camembert Eclairs with Walnut Butter 26
Little Chickens in Sauternes 136

INDEX

Little Tartlets of Field Mushroom Risotto with White Truffle Oil 30
Marbled Egg, Smoked Eel and Wasabi 48
Mayonnaise 182
Minted Lamb Tartlets with Soft Parmesan Crust 33
Monkfish with Lemon, Herbs and Vermouth 126
Mushroom Stock 184
Onion and Oxtail Soup 59
Orange Tabbouleh 129
Oranges in Champagne with Toffeed Strawberries 150
Peach Chutney 29
Peppered Scallop Bisque with Walnut Dumplings 56
Persian Meringue Cake with Stained Glass Sugar 146
Pistachio Chicken with Orange Mustard Sauce 65
Polenta Pudding with Blackberry Compôte and Mascarpone Cream 148
Pork with Rosemary and White Wine 131
Potted Hazelnut Cheese with Avocado and Grapefruit Salad 177
Pumpkin, Brie and Scallop Bisque with Prosciutto 57
Red Pepper and Pear Soup 61
Red Wine Confit with Green Garlic Souffle 70
Ricotta Pancakes with Sautéed Spiced Pears 168
Roulade of Saffron with Double-Cream Brie 38
Salad of Camembert with Mint, Peach and Ginger 100
Salad of Chicken with Tamarillo 90
Salad of Rare Beef with Pickled Walnuts and Horseradish 98
Salad of Roasted Vegetables in Yoghurt Pastry 110
Salad of Tomato, Roasted Garlic, Shallots and White Truffle Oil 94
Seafood Salad with Citrus Sorbet 87
Shank of Lamb with Red Wine and Gherkins 128
Sherried Fruit Sauce 160
Soup Almondine 58
Steeped Oranges with Green Ginger 156
Stilton Shortbread 169
Sweet French Dressing 182
Tabil 33
Tajine of Chicken with Summer Tomato Jam 118
Tartare of New Zealand Venison 34
Tartlet Base 181
Terrine of New Potato, Thyme and Double-Cream Brie with a Water Vinaigrette 68
Toasted Ravioli with Tomato Rosemary Sauce 72
Turban of Two Salmon with Gazpacho Dressing 92
Turkish Delight 172
Venison with Ginger and Pasta Rosti 114
Warm Marinated Salmon 47
Warm Mushroom Pâté with Apples and Cognac 46
White Chocolate Cake Soufflé with Tangerine Sauce 152
White Chocolate Fudge with Hazelnut Praline 176
White Wine and Cheese Fritters 32
Wine and Vegetable Stock 185